by the same author

THE COLLECTED PLAYS OF PETER BARNES
(Heinemann)

RED NOSES

PETER BARNES

faber and faber
LONDON · BOSTON

First published in 1985
by Faber and Faber Limited
3 Queen Square London WC1N 3AU

Photoset by Wilmaset Birkenhead Merseyside
Printed in Great Britain by
Redwood Burn Ltd Trowbridge Wiltshire

Words from the song 'Life is Just a Bowl of Cherries' by
Lew Brown and Ray Henderson on pages 14–15, are
reproduced by kind permission of Redwood Music Ltd.

All professional and amateur rights in this play are strictly
reserved and applications for permission to perform it must be
made in advance to Margaret Ramsay Ltd, 14a Goodwins Court,
London WC2N 4LL

British Library Cataloguing in Publication Data

Barnes, Peter, 1931–
Red noses
I. Title
822'.914   PR6052.A668
ISBN 0–571–13771–7

To Terry

INTRODUCTION

Red Noses was written in 1978. It has taken seven years for it to be produced, which is the same time it took Solomon to build his temple. The time lapse is not surprising. The reaction to *The Bewitched*, the last play of mine produced by the Royal Shakespeare Company, ranged roughly from 'someone should take an axe to the author for writing it', to 'someone should take the subsidy from the Company for producing it'. Of course I have selected two of the more favourable comments.

But it is all perfectly natural. I am in no way complaining, merely providing necessary information. For if *Red Noses* was written today – 1985 – it would be much less optimistic. The world has moved on in seven years, and not towards the light. Men and women can still be overcome by a sudden wave of compassion for the poor and sick but they quickly get over it, while the majority, it seems, find something deeply offensive about any transaction in which money does not change hands.

Red Noses is a letter from a transfigured world, much like ours, where statues come to life and human beings turn to stone. It's a letter wishing you good thoughts, but chiefly, good feelings.

PETER BARNES

CHARACTERS

VIENNET
MONCRIFF
EVALINE
BONVILLE
MADAME BONVILLE
DR ANTRECHAU
FLOTE
GREZ
SCARRON
DRUCE
SONNERIE
ARCHBISHOP MONSELET
FATHER TOULON
FIRST ATTENDANT
MISTRAL
BRODIN
ROCHFORT

MARGUERITE
LEFRANC
PELLICO
CAMILLE
MARIE
LE GRUE
BEMBO
FRAPPER
BOUTROS BROTHERS
VASQUES
BIGOD
SABINE
PATRIS
MOTHER METZ
PAPAL HERALD
POPE CLEMENT VI

FLAGELLANTS, PEASANTS, ARTISANS, PEDLARS, LEPERS, MONKS, ATTENDANTS AND GUARDS

Red Noses was first performed by the Royal Shakespeare Company at the Barbican Theatre on 2 July 1985. The cast included:

MOTHER METZ/	
MME DE BONVILLE	Yvonne Coulette
MARGUERITE	Polly James
CAMILLE	Rowena Roberts
MARIE	Katharine Rogers
SABINE	Cathy Tyson
POPE CLEMENT VI	Christopher Benjamin
ARCHBISHOP MONSELET	Raymond Bowers
BEMBO	Derek Crewe
ROCHFORT	Richard Easton
TOULON	Peter Eyre
GREZ	Nicholas Farrell
LEFRANC	Norman Henry
SONNERIE	Jim Hooper
LE GRUE	Bernard Horsfall
PELLICO	Don McKillop
BOUTROS ONE	Charles Millham
SCARRON	Brian Parr
BRODIN	Pete Postlethwaite
FLOTE	Antony Sher
PATRIS	Peter Theedom
BOUTROS TWO	David Whitaker
FRAPPER	Nicholas Woodeson
DRUCE	Jimmy Yuill
Other parts played by:	Nicholas Bell
	Phillip Dupuy
	James Newall
	Steve Swinscoe
Director	Terry Hands
Designer	Farrah
Music	Stephan Deutsch
Choreographer	Ben Benison
Lighting	Terry Hands and Clive Morris

ACT I

ONE

Auxerre, France. 1348. White mist. A bell tolls and a VOICE *calls,* 'Bring out your dead!' *Five plague victims stagger on Upstage Centre.* MONCRIFF *manically sniffs scent boxes,* VIENNET *tries to wrap himself in a winding sheet,* EVALINE *moans and* BONVILLE *beats a tiny drum for* MADAME BONVILLE *as she dances weakly.*

VIENNET: Out. Tear out these scabs. (*He tries to tear off the scabs on his arms.*) No pain here, pain's a sure sign of the pestilence.

MONCRIFF: Monday: wormwood, rosemary, marjoram. Tuesday: valerian, alant, juniper. Wednesday: red-fern, milfoil, lavender. They cure the plague if you sniff. I know, I've spent money.

VIENNET: I plead. *Durante bene placito.* In life, lawyers dress in black ready for the Diet of Worms.

EVALINE: Day's gone, night's here. Kneeled out my life asking forgiveness. A dead, dry branch.

BONVILLE: You served me old meat, Madam, that brings on the plague. Go dance and die.

MADAM BONVILLE: Drum, Maurice, drum. He's playing games with my bones. Run fast, run soon, return late is the only certain plague cure.
(*They collapse Upstage Centre as* DR ANTRECHAU *enters Upstage Left carrying a long stick and a document, which he reads aloud.*)

DR ANTRECHAU: The College of Physicians of Paris hereby make known the cause of pestilence, the scourge of God, known as the Black Death. It arose in India when the sun sucked up, *whoosh*, the Great Sea, in the form of white mist which turned corrupt. 'Twill continue as long as the sun's in the sign of Leo, they say.

BONVILLE: Help us, Dr Antrechau, Dr Antrechau.
(*The five crawl towards him. He holds them off with his stick.*)

DR ANTRECHAU: Stay back eight metres, else I catch the pestilence.

VIENNET: You read us the cause, read us the cure!

DR ANTRECHAU: I prescribe wine and they die, no wine and they die, exercise and they die, abstinence and they die, debauchery and they die, cold meat and they die, hot meat and they die, no meat and they die, sleep on the right side and they die, left side, ditto. I've a hundred per cent record of failure. All turn black and stinking.

(*A line of four cowled* MONKS *enters Downstage Right moaning rhythmically. As they cross to exit Stage Right the last one,* MARCEL FLOTE, *starts jerking convulsively and falls on his knees.*)

FLOTE: *Aa-ooh-aah*, light my way, Lord, show me what I must do. Trees wither, fixed stars fall, darkness swallows the world and the dead are no longer counted. Infection's everywhere and the people cry, 'O wicked God.' It came October last in the year of Our Saviour 1347. Twelve Genoese ships fleeing from Kaffa entered Messina carrying the buboes of the Black Death. Mercy, Lord. One third of Christendom now lies under sod. Men waking healthy are dead before noon, stripped and dragged to plague pits where they lie pickled like game in a barrel, quicklimed instead of salted. There's no pity, faith or love left, when the breath, touch or look of a loved one's pestilential, and suckling babes drink up death instead of mother's milk. Let me be chosen, Lord, to mend it. You came to me, Lord, in a street in Auxerre. Like Paul I was afflicted. I cried out *aa-ooh-aah*. (*He jerks violently.*) You spoke in my inner ear saying, 'I have work for thee, Marcel – wait.' I still wait, waiting, Lord, for a sign so I may begin. What would you have me do, Lord? I thirst for it. Speak Lord, let me hear again the voice of Him who made the world, *aa-ooh-aah*.

(*Whips are heard cracking loudly as two* FLAGELLANTS *enter Downstage Right, hitting themselves with clubs. They are half naked, with iron bands round their waists and foreheads.* GREZ, *the Master of Flagellants, in a black coat with a red cross, walks alongside.*)

FLAGELLANTS: (*Chanting*) 'Pain, pain, pain. Our journey's done in holy name. Christ himself to Calvary came. Pain, pain,

pain. Mary's honour free from stain. Repent and do not sin
again. Pain, pain, pain.'

GREZ: Ave Maria, sweet Mother Mary, hear the plea of thy
servant Grez, Master of Flagellants. Have pity on us. Rise,
O Heaven, let Christ's black anger for our sins be appeased
by this bloody sacrifice. Let our penitential scourging take
away God's pestilential wrath. We feel Christ's thorns,
whips, nails and spear, that we may be freed of sin and
death. Join us, Brother. Join us on this painful pilgrimage.

FLOTE: I come,brother, *aa-ooh-aah*.

(*He gets up, jerking, and crosses to* GREZ, *who hands him a
club.*)

GREZ: Welcome to the Brotherhood of Pain, Brother.

FLOTE: *Aa-ooh-aah*.

(*Jerking violently, he inadvertently cracks the club down on*
GREZ's *head.* GREZ *groans and falls to his knees.*)

GREZ: No, Brother, you hit yourself for Christ's sake, not me.

FLOTE: *Aa-ooh-aah*.

(FLOTE *has another spasm and hits* GREZ *again as he tries to
get up. Grunting with pain,* GREZ *deliberately takes a club
from his waist, rises slowly and hammers* FLOTE *over the head
with it.*)

GREZ: And *aa-ooh-aah* to you too.

(FLOTE *grunts and clubs* GREZ *back. The two hit each other
with increasing fury, as they slowly sink to their knees.
Suddenly* FLOTE *holds up his hand.* GREZ *stops hitting him.
They both listen to an unaccustomed sound: the* FLAGELLANTS
are actually laughing at them. As they scramble up, FLOTE
becomes entangled in GREZ's *cloak. More laughter; even the*
PLAGUE VICTIMS *upstage manage to smile.* GREZ *finally
untangles himself.*) Blasphemous clown! (*He signals furiously
to the* FLAGELLANTS. *They exit Stage Right laughing with*
DR ANTRECHAU. FLOTE *looks after them, then falls on his
knees.*)

FLOTE: I hear you loud, Lord, in the sound of their laughter. I
hear and obey. I now know what I must do. Heaven's to be
had with my humiliation. God wants peacocks not ravens,
bright stars not sad comets, red noses not black death. He

wants joy. I'll not shrink from the burden, Lord. Only turn away thy wrath. Give us hope.

(*He rises and crosses to the* PLAGUE VICTIMS.)

EVALINE: The light is dying! They take away the light, the light of the world.

VIENNET: (*Drinking from a bottle*) This water's dead. This is dead water.

MONCRIFF: I begin to ooze.

MADAM BONVILLE: Lord've mercy, what night is this night?

BONVILLE: I rake my ashes.

MONCRIFF: I hear worms.

(FLOTE *touches the crouching* MONCRIFF *who topples over dead.*)

FLOTE: So . . . so . . . (*He gently closes* MONCRIFF's *eyes.*) In nomine Patris . . .

VIENNET: Aren't you frightened?

FLOTE: I'm so frightened the water on my knee's splashing. I feel like Philip the Fair's new jester, Bosco Gide. 'Make me laugh, Bosco, or I'll rack and bastinade you,' said Philip. 'Sire, sire, my wife's dying, my six children're starving, my house's burnt down and I've lost all my money. I've nothing left. Spare me! Spare me!' 'Heee-heeee-hee, that's very good, Bosco, you're hired,' spluttered Philip. (*He puts on a clown's bulbous red nose and sings:*) 'Don't make it serious. Life's too mysterious. You work, you pray, you worry so. But you can't take your gold when you go, go, go . . .' Did you know your navel is a useful place to keep salt when you're eating celery in bed? (*Singing*) 'So keep repeating it's the berries. The strongest oak must fall. The sweet things in life to you were just loaned.' . . . Simon went to heaven. 'How did you get here?' asked St Peter. Simon sneezed and said, 'Flu . . .'

VIENNET: Flu! The final degradation, to face life's supreme test surrounded by an incompetent clown.

FLOTE: I know. But tell me, Master Viennet, is it true lawyers believe all men innocent till proved penniless?

(VIENNET *stares at him, lets out a thin, whinnying laugh and dies.* EVALINE *clutches at* FLOTE, *who takes her hand.*)

EVALINE: Are there still young men outside? Is it wrong to love?

FLOTE: The commandment is, love thy neighbour only don't get caught doing it. (EVALINE *smiles and falls back.*)
(FLOTE *singing*) 'Life is just a bowl of cherries . . .'

MADAM BONVILLE: Father, Father!

FLOTE: Did you hear about old Dubois? He told the marriage broker he wouldn't marry the girl without a sample of her sexual powers. 'No samples,' said the girl, 'but references he can have . . .' (*Singing*) 'So live and laugh at it all.'
(MADAM BONVILLE *stops dancing, shakes with laughter and collapses.*)

BONVILLE: She's dead. There's nothing I wouldn't have done for her and nothing she wouldn't have done for me. So we ended up doing nothing for each other.

FLOTE: But swallows always fly in pairs and mandarin ducks never roost apart.

BONVILLE: My thanks, Father Flote, it's easy finding someone to share your life, but who'll share your death?
(*He curls up, coughs and dies.* FLOTE *makes the sign of the cross over the dead.*)

FLOTE: The immortal souls of men and women who dwelled on land, change into birds after death they say. Fly, fly my sweet souls, fly, fly to heaven. And I must fly too to see the Bishop, if he's still to be found in Auxerre. (*Singing softly*) 'Yes, life is just a bowl of cherries, so love and laugh at it all.'
(*Two corpse-bearers,* SCARRON *and* DRUCE, *dressed in black hoods and smocks painted with white crosses and carrying long, forked poles, enter Stage Left, 'cawing' harshly.* DRUCE *puts on gloves to search the bodies before they use their poles to slide them off, Stage Right.*)

SCARRON: Run, spit-gobs, run. The corpse bearers, the Black Ravens have come, *caw-caw.*

DRUCE: These mouldering scrag ends got nothing worth stealing.
(SCARRON *takes out two small bottles and hands one to* DRUCE.)

SCARRON: There's always something worth stealing. The boils,

15

the wet plague boils are worth stealing. Squeeze. Squeeze 'em.

(*As they squeeze the pus from the boils on the corpses and into the bottles,* FLOTE *joins them.*)

FLOTE: What are you doing, friends?

SCARRON: We need more plague pus. Plague pus mixed with aconite and napellum makes the best killing grease.

DRUCE: Tonight we grease silver spoons, brass door handles, jewelled crucifixes, anything lace-soft fingers touch, full lips kiss.

SCARRON: As their lives were made easy with riches, so their deaths're made easy with grease.

FLOTE: But they are still men like you.

SCARRON: No, we're not men, we're Black Ravens – corpse bearers. And before that galley slaves and before that serfs. We've always been poor, never men. Don't call us men now because it suits.

FLOTE: But why do you grease?

DRUCE: Every one we grease dead means . . . Jesu, this old un's still breathing . . . (*He takes a small cudgel from his belt and kills* MADAM BONVILLE) . . . an extra two denari plus pickings. The rich are the richest pickings, so we grease the rich.

SCARRON: That's not it at all. We grease for a higher purpose, to wipe the slate clean, turn the world underside up, crack the Universe. We grease because we hate. I travelled through my life in the world's bowels like Jonah in the dark fish. Now I'll stride into sunlight palaces. Grease the fat bellies out.

DRUCE: (*Examining* EVALINE's *body*) Here's a fine white ewe, swan-necked and soft all down. Lookee, she's flashing dead eyes at me. She's got thighs.

SCARRON: War, famine, pestilence, the world's dying only to be born again. Just as the seed corn rots in order to sprout and bear good fruit, so mankind must stink to flower in glory. Salvation's built on putrefaction. Plague time heralds a new dawn sun rising in the West. But we must seize the day not the nearest piece of tit-and-arse Hell-bait.

FLOTE: I'll pray for you.

SCARRON: Don't. We are the darkness.

FLOTE: Poor darkness. I've always felt sorry for the darkness.

SCARRON: *Caw-caw.*

(*As they slide* EVALINE's *body off and exit after it Stage Right,* DRUCE *sings sweetly.*)

DRUCE: (*Singing*) 'Stay lady, stay, join lips to mine as pigeons do. Thy body's marble-white but soft to touch and sweet to view. Death cannot take thee, let him wait. For thy sweeter smiling grace. I suck thee back, on thy flat belly roam. And plunder thy full honeycomb.'

FLOTE: Lord, I have not begun yet and am already cast down. I know the real sin of the Israelites in the desert was not their re ellion against God but their despair. (*He kneels.*) Lord, I kneel and stand upright, dance and remain motionless, shout and am silent all at the same time. But still I tremble at the burden. I dreamed I was leaning on a cane near a river and the river was a river of tears, tears of all the people suffering and dying everywhere. Must I cross the river alone? Solitude is welcome but loneliness is hard to bear. I'm on the road, Lord. Speak to me again. Blind me even as you did Paul, shake the earth, crush it in thunder, split it with raging fire . . . I look, I listen . . . (*There is the sound of tiny bells.*) Bells? Who asked for bells? Since when did God speak with bells? (SONNERIE *enters Upstage Right, his costume covered with tiny silver bells which ring gently. He crosses to* FLOTE *and bows gracefully.*) And good day to you too. (*He rises.*) I am sorry I was talking to God. (SONNERIE *shakes his right leg.*) Yes, it is quite common nowadays . . . I'm Father Flote. Who are you? (SONNERIE *jumps, shaking his left leg.*) Ah yes, a beautiful name, most fitting . . . (SONNERIE *shakes his right arm.*) No, I haven't heard of you before. I'm sorry but I have been busy – the plague . . . (SONNERIE *improvises a little dance;* FLOTE *laughs.*) Yes indeed . . . Very wittily put . . . Master Sonnerie, I am a fool! I mean, I am a fool for not seeing it before. You are the sign sent by God. Christ can use you, sweet Sonn. (SONNERIE *shakes his body.*) No, I offer nothing except

17

humility's tears. Peter cried, 'Oh thou shall never wash my feet,' and Christ answered, 'If I wash thee not thou hast no part of me.' There's no reward except laughter for His name's sake. Do you wish to join me, Master Bells, sweet Master Bells?

(SONNERIE *looks at him for a moment, then suddenly leaps into the air, shaking arms, legs and body.* FLOTE *laughs delightedly. They embrace and* FLOTE *presents him with a clown's red nose.* SONNERIE *bows, as* ARCHBISHOP MONSELET *rushes in Upstage Centre, accompanied by* FATHER TOULON *with papers and a* FIRST ATTENDANT *carrying a bowl of vinegar.*)

MONSELET: I'm leaving, Father Toulon, eternity's growing on my flesh. The rim and centre's breaking. Seven Cardinals, including the noble Giovanni Colunna and one hundred and five bishops're already plague-pitted, plague-dead. So in return they hang two scrawny Jews. Those were the only two left for slaughter. That's the size of the problem.

(TOULON *dips a parchment into the bowl of vinegar and hands it, dripping wet, to* MONSELET, *who reads it with difficulty.*)

TOULON: Live Jews haven't caused it, dead Jews can't cure it. The plague's but the inflammation of our sins – greed, wantonness, pride, blasphemy, despair, doing evil because it is evil. We die only to live in Hell's devouring flames.

MONSELET: You're such a comfort, Father. (*He stuffs the wet parchment into the* FIRST ATTENDANT'*s pouch as* TOULON *dips another document into the vinegar and hands it to him.*) Wet it! Wet, wet with vinegar! Vinegar's a protection against infection. Kills off the winged plague worms. (*He whips out a wooden fly-swatter and hits the air.*) Plague worms! Plague worms! Is it any wonder we sin? God sleeps and Satan's a mighty Prince, ever active. He grows. Have I chosen the wrong side? The losing side.

(FLOTE *and* SONNERIE *approach.*)

FLOTE: Reverend Father, I've come to see you.

MONSELET: Stay back! You haven't been vinegared. Back eight metres. (*He hits out with his swatter.*) I see wingy plague worms.

FLOTE: Most Reverend Father, I'm Father Flote and this is . . .
(SONNERIE *shakes his right leg.*)

MONSELET: God be with you, Master Bells.

FLOTE: Forgive me if I stand amazed, Reverend Father.
Everyone expected you to flee with the rest of the clergy.

MONSELET: *Arrrx*, you hear that, Toulon? Everyone expected
me to flee. You said everyone expected me to stay. I risk
buboes and plague worms for you. (*He hits* TOULON
savagely with his swatter.) Zealot. Fanatic. It's no good
giving you a penance. You enjoy doing without things.
Damnable conscience keeper. If I die, I'll kill you. What do
you want of me?

FLOTE: Only your approval, Reverend Father, I've been chosen
to go out to cheer the hearts of men with gibs, jibes and
jabber jinks. On the Octave of the Epiphany we hold the
Feast of Fools when the Mass is brayed and water poured
over the clergy at Vespers. I'll hold a daily Fools' Feast.
With thy blessing others'll join. We'll form a brotherhood
of joy, Christ's Clowns, God's Zanies – that's us, the Red
Noses of Auxerre.
(SONNERIE *rings the bells on his right and left arm at*
MONSELET.)

MONSELET: So, Master Bells, you say he heard God speak. But
nowadays every Tommy Tom-Turd man hears God
booming out of every stunted bush and passing cloud.
There are too many footloose clerics about like you, Father
Flote, preaching indiscriminate Christianity. It's natural
with whole congregations dead and the . . . DEAD, you hear
me? I could be dying even as I say this! Dead before I end
this speech! Kill the plague worms! Vinegar the air! Yet
Flote's Noses could be useful to the Church. The people'd
see there's no panic in the Temple of God. But the Holy
Father, Pope Clement, must give formal confirmation.

TOULON: Most Reverend Father, is this wise?

MONSELET: I don't have to be wise, just decisive.

TOULON: But laughter's the very pip of Eve's green apple. We
must suffer to be saved and dare not weaken God's anger,
die soft. (*He produces a Bible.*) There are no laughs in this

book, 'cept God's *haaa-haaa* roaring in His triumph, *haaa-haaa*. 'The Lord shall laugh at him for he seeth His day coming!' Psalm 37. Not the laughter of fools, cackling thorns under the pot *eeee-heee-heee*. But God's bloody laughter *haaa-haaa* roaring in his triumph, *haaa-haaa* not *heee-heee*.

FIRST ATTENDANT: *Hoo-hooo-ooooh* (*He pours the bowl of vinegar over his head and shrieks.*) I've got the boils, the black buboes! I'm stricken. (*The others shrink back.*) Mother of God, I'm not ready. I've only just been born and now I have to die. All the fault of writers – cock-pimping scribblers. They've prepared the way. Always writing stories where some characters are important and others just disposable stock – First Attendant, Second Peasant, Third Guard. Stories're easier when 'tisn't possible to care for everyone equal. That's how itty-bitty-bit people like me come to be butchered on battlefields, die in droves on a *hoo-hooo-ooooh*. But we First Attendants are important too. We've lives. I've lodged in the chaffinch, lived in the flower, seen the sun coming up. I've discovered unbelievable things. I'm an extraordinary person. I'll tell you a secret . . .
(*He dies.* SCARRON *and* DRUCE *enter quickly Upstage Centre and hook him off with them whilst* MONSELET *tries to grab* TOULON *round the throat to strangle him.*)

MONSELET: Judas priest, because of you I'm exposed to that! Flote, you've my permission to continue and multiply. I don't care if you collect red noses or black buboes.

TOULON: Your Grace, this fatuous Father could endanger the Church like the heretical Beghards, Beguines and buggering Bogomils who've been taken in Cambrai, Paris and Orléans. Now here in Auxerre I see another heresy being born – Flotism, the damnable heresy of happiness!

MONSELET: It's why you're staying, Father, to see he doesn't fall from orthodoxy into snout-deep error. Obey and suffer. You're to be one of Flote's Noses, *hee-hee-hee*.

TOULON: Crush, whip, scourge, crucify, only spare me this shame.

20

MONSELET: Not here to discuss. The plague worms won't survive snowy peaks so I'll go to the mountains, St-Jean or Montrecon.

FLOTE: I hate mountains, they spoil the view.

(TOULON *grabs* MONSELET *round his legs and is dragged across the floor.*)

TOULON: I can't let you go, you betray Christ with this cowardice.

MONSELET: Peter betrayed him thrice *cock-a-doodle-do, cock-a-doodle-do, cock-a-do-doodle.* My cowardice is transformed from inside by being practised with a religious fervour. Nothingness is at my back!

(*He kicks* TOULON *off and exits quickly, ducking and weaving, Stage Right.* TOULON *gets up.*)

TOULON: The first duty of a Priest is obedience. So I must become a Nose. (FLOTE *shakes his head.*) Don't shake your head at me in that tone of voice. (SONNERIE *gently waves his arm in front of* FLOTE's *ear.*) Why are you whispering?

FLOTE: Before you can join Christ's Clowns, Father, you must prove of use.

TOULON: Use? A man of my moral inflexibility would be welcomed with open arms in any religious community.

FLOTE: First we must ask, can you play a tune on your head like Sasha Gelen, 'the man with the musical skull', or by rubbing your knees together like Perri Rouve, the Human Grasshopper? Can you play the hubble-bubble buffoon, the capering roach and simkin? Can you make them roar with a quip that brings the roses back to their elbows?

TOULON: Insolent priest, I only smiled once in my life and then my face slipped. No, I can't play a tune on my head, rub my knees together, caper or quip.

FLOTE: Then you can't be a Red Nose.

TOULON: But I can't not be. I have my orders, eyes front, quick march.

(SONNERIE *shakes his body excitedly.*)

FLOTE: That's right, sweet Sonn. We can teach you, so Christ can use you, Father Toulon.

(SONNERIE *repeatedly hits himself on the head with a rubber hammer whilst* FLOTE *bangs his knees together and hands him a clown's red nose.* TOULON *looks at it and shudders.*)

TOULON: Let us pray for God's help and protection.

FLOTE: I've already done that, Father.

TOULON: Not for you, for me!

(*As they pray intently in the shadows Upstage, there is a cry as* BRODIN *and* MISTRAL *rush in Downstage Left, bristling with swords and dragging a screaming Nun,* MARGUERITE DELAIR, *and followed by* CHARLES ROCHFORT *in an old suit of armour, nibbling a roast chicken. They throw* MARGUERITE *down screaming.*)

MISTRAL: We divvy up equal 'cept I get to rape this Holy Wagtail first.

BRODIN: If it's equal why do you get to rape her first?

MISTRAL: 'Cause I'm the leader.

BRODIN: Why're you the leader?

MISTRAL: 'Cause I get to rape her first. It's logic.

BRODIN: There's no logic in our breaking world, no leaders either. What we get, we get by force. What we keep, we keep by force. If you can't keep it, you've no right to it.

MISTRAL: Raping nuns is my habit. Stand back, Brodin, I've killed more men than you've had hot dinners.

ROCHFORT: And I know how – you ran 'em to death.

BRODIN: Defend yourself, crotch-bag. I give you ten seconds to draw a sword. One, two, three, four, five, six, seven, eight, nine, ten.

(*As* MISTRAL *starts to unsheath his sword,* BRODIN *whips out his dagger and stabs him in the stomach.*)

MISTRAL: I'm stained. You was too quick. Foul! Foul!

(ROCHFORT *tosses him a chicken leg.*) Dying over a nothing . . . one hole for another . . . bones of cuttlefish, embers of once bright stars . . . when I was young I blew soap bubbles from a reed . . . (ROCHFORT *mimes blowing soap bubbles.*) See how they float light . . . (*He tries stabbing one with his forefinger.*) You've taken all my days, Brodin. Done for me . . . (*He falls to his knees.*) My name's Jean Mistral! Jean Mistral! Jean Mistral!

(*The name comes back in a loud echo.*)

ECHO: Jean Mistral! Jean Mistral! Jean Mistral! (*Satisfied, he pitches forward dead.* BRODIN *stands over him and sniffs loudly.*)

BRODIN: I draw up his strength.

ROCHFORT: Do try not to kill without being paid, Brodin. It lowers the market value of our work.

BRODIN: The avenging angel circles like the sun and men and women strike each other down; it's natural. So without a war it's natural we war against ourselves.

ROCHFORT: Salt. Where's the salt? This bird's not properly salted. Women never make good cooks, they aren't generous enough. My father's house had cooks. Boiled porcupine and wild boar.

BRODIN: It's your damn Master Pestilence. Remember we had a good war going – a hundred years, nothing less. Then this pestilence comes on by and it's over. Now instead of war and killing we got peace and dying. Peace?! Peace?!

ROCHFORT: Who won the battle of Crécy, Brodin? I was there, but nobody told me who won.

BRODIN: They say the English bowmen won. Arrows and spears wet with blood, drums toppled, standards broken, riderless horses lost amongst the dead. We fertilized the ground with our flesh but I don't rightly know who won.

ROCHFORT: Chivalry lost I know. All lost when Robert of Artois fell at Coutroi asking for honourable quarter and a low-born pikeman cut his throat saying, 'Sorry, I don't speak French.'

(BRODIN *stops sniffing the body and* DRUCE *and* SCARRON *enter quickly Stage Left and hook* MISTRAL's *corpse off with them as* BRODIN *unbuckles his belt.*)

BRODIN: Now for the Holy Wagtail. One thrust made me a dead 'un, another thrust could make me a live 'un. Rut, Sister! Rut!

(*He grabs* MARGUERITE *who starts screaming again causing* FLOTE, SONNERIE *and* TOULON *finally to stop praying Upstage and come forward.*)

FLOTE: If you attack that Bride of Christ, I'll stand here and make uncouth noises with my mouth. The Church can't stop you sinning but it can stop you enjoying it.

TOULON: Remember, the pleasure's transitory, the price excessive, the position ridiculous.

(BRODIN *picks up* MISTRAL's *sword and thrusts it into* FLOTE's *belt.*)

BRODIN: Defend yourself, priest. I give you ten seconds to draw a sword. One, two, three, four, five . . .

(FLOTE *whips out a crayon and parchment and quickly draws on it.* BRODIN *slowly turns to the audience and looks heavenwards.*)

FLOTE: Six, seven, eight, nine, ten. It's done. (*He hands the sketch to* BRODIN.) Gitto couldn't've drawn a better sword in ten seconds.

BRODIN: You bacon-faced gullion, I'll . . . (*Looking at the drawing*) Phswk. Call that a sword? You don't know a sword from a ploughshare. Give me that crayon.

(*He starts sketching on the other side of the parchment as* MARGUERITE *finally scrambles up.*)

MARGUERITE: I'm supposed to be raped! What of the raping, spindle-shanks? I was promised marauding prickmen. There'll be atrocities, they said. Rape and ravaging, they said. I want to be first.

BRODIN: I'm not in the raping mood. Raping means taking a woman by force. You're giving it free.

ROCHFORT: I've never been given anything free by a woman. I always found I had to pay for it one way or another in the end.

(MARGUERITE *snatches the fowl from him.*)

MARGUERITE: Salt. Did you say it needed salt? I cooked it, addle-pate. If you don't like it, don't eat it. Five years of prayers and going to bed with a night light and misgivings and I can't even get raped.

TOULON: You're pledged to service God not men, Sister.

MARGUERITE: The violation of my body's but another penance, Father. Saint Bartholomew was whipped, I raped.

(BRODIN *finishes the drawing and shows it to* SONNERIE, FLOTE *and* TOULON. FLOTE *compares the two drawings.*)

FLOTE: Yes . . .

ROCHFORT: I find it a major work utterly convincing in its palpable use of physical existence . . . (SONNERIE *shakes his legs*.) And that too.

BRODIN: Drawing is in my blood as well as killing. (*He starts another sketch*.) I've got the hands for it.

MARGUERITE: When I was young I had my plum tree shook twice nightly. Now you can't find the men for it. That dead one . . . what was his name? (MISTRAL'S VOICE *is heard calling* 'Jean Mistral! Jean Mistral!') Yes, Jean Mistral. He was going to try but he fell back into shadow. (*She sits*.) Life is so insulting. I'll never smile again.

(SONNERIE *dances in front of her*.)

ROCHFORT: I know that song, Master Bells.

(*He takes out a flute and plays*. MARGUERITE *jumps up*.)

MARGUERITE: So do I. (*Singing*) 'With an Oh and Oh, she itching moves her hips. And to and fro she lightly starts and skips. She jerks her legs and sprawleth out her heels. Oh what's this joy, a man and woman feels.'

FLOTE: Christ can use you. And you, gentle fluter. (BRODIN *shows him his drawing*.) And, yes, you with the lightning hands. (*He takes three coloured balls from a bag and juggles with them*.) God's ordered me to found a new order without orders, bound by no authority except love. We'll work together in singleness of heart, joining hands with Christ to lift fear from Creation. These balls are God, *ally-oop*. (*Without breaking rhythm he passes the balls to* MARGUERITE *who continues juggling*.) Feel Him, *ally-oop ally-oop*.

MARGUERITE: I feel Him!

(*Still juggling she passes them on to* SONNERIE *who passes them on to* BRODIN.)

BRODIN: They're strong and hard, a soldier's balls. We'll take time out from killing and fight Master Pestilence.

(*Still juggling he passes them on to* ROCHFORT.)

ROCHFORT: And boredom, which is worse. I fear boredom more than death and repetition more than sin. So long as the balls amuse, I'll follow. What do you want us to be, Father – poor Friars, rich Templars, suffering Saints?

(SONNERIE *jumps up shaking his head and ringing his bells in reply.*)

MARGUERITE, BRODIN and ROCHFORT: Clowns?! You want us to be *clowns*?!

(ROCHFORT *drops the balls in astonishment and* TOULON *catches them all first bounce in the bag and snaps it shut.*)

TOULON: Flote, you're preaching vile equality and love again. Look at 'em. One blood-soaked beserker, one renegade chicken-eating aristo and a nun waiting to be raped as a penance. Three fools don't signify and a thousand fools only turn one righteous man into another fool. How do you know God is interested in our laughter and joy? Perhaps He wants our tears and suffering? I *know* He wants our tears and suffering. I stand with one foot in Heaven and the other gloriously in the abyss. Compromise is for the weak, concessions for cowards. I never yield or compromise. I obey. Obedience is the first vow of religion. Our task shouldn't be to make them smile, make them sleep easier in their beds, but to make them tremble. The link between God and man, man and man, is fear. God wants to be feared not loved. Make them bow down and tremble.

FLOTE: If that is life, I don't want it. I'll go through it as a stranger, curl up and die. If that is man, what's the good of saving him? But he is more and God is more. He can be moved by joy as well as tears. Come, friends, first we ask permission of the Goldmerchants' Guild to put on a show of our clowning art in the Goldmerchants' Square, Auxerre, this Eastertide. Then we send out a call for all those Red Nose Zanies waiting in green nooks and dark corners. We'll sing, dance and tell funny tales and all around us people will laugh and up there in Paradise the saints will interrupt their endless hosannas and laugh too. And the angels will forget their nocturnal missions and flutter their wings and chuckle the while. And the Judges of the Last Judgement will have to stop their judging for they will be chortling with glee. And the Supreme Judge himself will turn aside from sad pleas and soul-breaking prayers to hear the unfamiliar sound of joy and, perhaps, He will forget His

wrath hearing His people praise Him in laughter,
aaa-ooh-aah.

(*He jerks violently but immediately converts his jerkings into a soft-shoe shuffle. The others to join in as large, gold-paper butterflies are lowered from the Flies.*)

TWO

They stop dancing and FLOTE *is left gazing up entranced at the golden butterflies as* LEFRANC *and* PELLICO *enter singing Stage Right dressed in long black fur-trimmed coats and gold chains and pushing a huge mountain of gold on wheels.*

LEFRANC and PELLICO: (*Singing*) 'Gold, gold, gold. Bright and
    yellow, never cold. Molten, graven, hammered, rolled.
    Hard to get and good to hold. Gold, gold, gold.'
    (*They bow to the gold mountain.*)
LEFRANC: Great luminary keystone of the world's arch, symbol
    of heaven's highway, incorruptible metal. We declare this,
    the twenty-fourth meeting of the Auxerre Goldmerchants'
    Guild, now open. Though they lived by the golden rule –
    those that have the gold make the rules – Guildmasters
    Renard, Frogues, and Dubry have all met their death day.
    The burn-boils, the Black Death buboes!
PELLICO: We Guildmerchants Pellico and Lefranc are the only
    two left living out of four hundred. Suddenly the world is
    cold, and we are mortal, despite our gold.
    (*As* FLOTE *is still staring up in wonder at the gold butterflies,*
    TOULON *steps forward to introduce the others.*)
TOULON: Master Pellico, Master Lefranc, we . . .
LEFRANC: Father, this is a private meeting of the
    Goldmerchants' Guild. As a special dispensation you can
    watch but you mustn't interrupt the solemn proceedings.
TOULON: But we've urgent business.
PELLICO: Later, Father, first can you make sense of it all? We
    Merchants are the best. Creators of wealth, employers of
    labour, owners of property. Frugal and sober, we wore
    modest colours, kept strict ledgers, bolted our doors early.
    Money was our stout buttress, maximum intensity of greed
    our first principle. Such goodness worthless against this
    pestilence.
LEFRANC: That's why we had to change to stay alive. Instead of

thrift we waste, instead of working, we debauch like little
Neros. Pleasure's the best plague cure, voluptuousness and
excess will prolong our lives, cu, ca, po, fo.
(*As they wave* TOULON *and the others back and throw off their
coats to show they are dressed in brightly coloured jerkins,
striped breeches and golden codpieces,* CAMILLE *and* MARIE
enter Stage Right stamping and chanting.)

CAMILLE and MARIE: Cu, ca, po, fo.

LEFRANC: Oh a good set of dairies and buttocks is better
medicine than all your plague cordials, ointments and
charms.

PELLICO: Whores, whores, must have me some whores, wanna
kiss the whores. My pego's bigger than a mule's, stouter
than a bull's, so long you just put it in and walk towards
me. Whores, whores, wanna kiss the whores.

CAMILLE: We've business to discuss first. (*She hands each man a
list.*) Our new plague rates for whoring as sanctioned by the
Whores' Guild of Auxerre. Fees for all one hundred and
twenty-four ways of threading: back, front, singles,
doubles, triples and the rest.

PELLICO: (*Reading*) 'Twenty-two denari for the missionary
position'? The whoremaster who wrote this must've had his
tongue in his cheek and every other orifice. I just hope I can
raise my peg as high as your prices.

CAMILLE: Yer getting the *crème de la crème* certified free of all
infection. The Whores' Guild still keeps up standards.
(*Singing*) 'Oh Blessed Virgin we believe, that thou without
sin didst conceive. Teach us then how thus believing, we
can sin without conceiving.'

MARIE: If yer want *à-la-carte* humping, yer have to pay for it.

LEFRANC: We'll pay for it with pleasure.

CAMILLE: With pleasure it'll cost you more.

LEFRANC: Here's socket money. (*He opens his codpiece and
money falls out.*) There's four hundred for night on night till
this long night's ended and the plague worms' blister dead.
Kneel, Marie, Queen o' Heaven, Handmaiden of Joy. I
clothe thee with the sun.
(*As* MARIE *kneels,* LEFRANC *pours gold dust over her.*)

MARIE: I've gone down on the stiffest coral-headed pleasure-tube, squeezed the plumpest jingle-jobs. Money's better. Smooth, hot, hard, my darling gold. Let me kiss thee, roll thee between my apples, slip thee between my thighs, *aarr*.

PELLICO: Lefranc, Lefranc, I try but I can't forget, that's Guild gold yer spilling. Dead members' fees; years of graft and cheating there.

MARIE: Cheap at the price for in our arms you'll come like the animals, rut your way to life.

CAMILLE: Stags and stallions empty it in one short thunderclap, goats and buck rabbits six times hourly, leeches do it to themselves and elephants can bugger an ant given enough time and patience. Pigs grunt, *grrr grrr*, vultures groan inside dead carcasses, *urrr urrr*, frogs ride twenty days at a time, *huhh huhh*. *Grrr grrr, urrr urrr, huhh huhh.*

(CAMILLE *and* MARIE *leap on* LEFRANC *and* PELLICO, *twining their arms and legs round them. They jerk about grunting loudly.*)

TOULON: The pestilence has sent 'em mad. See, death thrusts hard.

BRODIN: 'Taint death thrusting but life.

TOULON: Humped-backed crotch-thumpers! I cannot keep silent whilst you wallow in this disease of nature, honeyed poison, body's bane, soul's perdition – lust, mere lust.

ROCHFORT: I've always found mere lust very agreeable – its pleasure is so short. Anything longer would be tedious.

MARGUERITE: I should've been told sooner. This isn't a private meeting, it's a public orgy!

TOULON: Stay, Sister Marguerite, remember thy holy calling.

MARGUERITE: Rahab was a harlot, Bethseba leaped into bed with her husband's murderer and from those holy loins sprang the holy line of Jesus. I want to join those divine bawds. Forward with me!

(CAMILLE *and* MARIE *drop off* LEFRANC *and* PELLICO.)

CAMILLE: Not unless you've got a fully paid-up Guild card you can't.

MARGUERITE: I'm coming!

CAMILLE: If you come, we don't. This is a professional hump. No scabs allowed 'cept those got in the line of duty. And with all due respect, which ain't much, it'll cost you peepers fifteen denari for the privilege of watching.

(MARIE *crosses to* BRODIN *who has been sketching*.)

MARIE: And what've you been doing with your hands? (*She looks at the drawing.*) I'm broad-minded to the point of obscenity but that's filthy.

PELLICO: Filthy? I'll take six copies.

TOULON: We'll not pay fifteen denari to watch sin, madam.

MARIE: When I was Brothel Queen in the Vatican Whorehouse, we charged twenty. Of course, you pay for style.

ROCHFORT: I've always looked down on whores, usually through a hole in the ceiling.

CAMILLE: Master Bells, you got bells all over? Never had it with bells. (SONNERIE *sensuously shakes his body*.) Really. . . ? That sounds different.

PELLICO: Come, let's get to the humping.

CAMILLE: Sorry, Master Bells, I have to work.

(CAMILLE *and* MARIE *are about to jump on* LEFRANC *and* PELLICO *again*.)

TOULON: Father Flote, are you still with this company or are you just going to stand there using up air?

FLOTE: I was looking at the butterflies and thinking we are in Paradise.

PELLICO: No, this is supposed to be the twenty-fourth meeting of the Goldmerchants' Guild.

FLOTE: Why butterflies?

LEFRANC: Devices to shift the plague worms from the stagnant air.

(*He gestures and the paper butterflies flap their wings*.)

FLOTE: Ah, they enchant, friend.

TOULON: We've no time for idle chatter, tongueless talk, there's business to discuss.

LEFRANC: Not in business. Death's put an end to business.

FLOTE: We're Christ's Clowns and we wish to use Goldmerchants' Square for a public display this Easter Monday.

TOULON: Here's ten denari to seal the bond.

LEFRANC: Money's lost its value, salt its flavour, we're for pleasure.

FLOTE: Ravished by joy, we'll give you pleasure on Easter morning. A show to dazzle and delight.

(*There is a loud whip crack and* GREZ *and two* FLAGELLANTS *lurch in Upstage Centre.*)

GREZ: Blood, ravished by blood! My blood, their blood, our blood, God's blood. It's the salvation of blood.

CAMILLE: Who's this loon? Somebody must be giving away free tickets.

MARIE: Whips'll cost you more. (GREZ *hits himself.*) Would you like me to do that for you? Twenty denari, special offer.

LEFRANC: Sirs, this is a monthly meeting of the Goldmerchants' Guild. Non-members are simply not allowed. Have you no sense of occasion?

GREZ: We sought Pope Clement in Avignon, found him a sucking dog-leech selling Christ's cross and flesh for profit. His court is a stinking bank of usury. We say no man need go to Avignon or Hell to find Pope or Devil. Both lodge in his own breast. We shall proclaim it this Easter morn in Goldmerchants' Square, Auxerre.

FLOTE: The square is ours, Master Grez.

TOULON: No double bookings!

PELLICO: I'm an old man, just want to dip my dildo. Just want to lie bell-clapper to belly.

LEFRANC: Gold we've got, humping we want – debauch! debauch!

(CAMILLE *and* MARIE *leap on* LEFRANC *and* PELLICO *again and they jerk around grunting.* GREZ *stabs his thigh repeatedly with a knife.*)

GREZ: On Easter Monday in the square in Auxerre we'll denounce false world, false Church. We're Christ's red meat, hacked raw. They that sow in tears shall reap in joy. Closest to Him when speared, flayed, racked.

FLOTE: On Easter Monday in the square in Auxerre we'll put on a honey-pellet show that'll set the toes a tap-tap-tapping. Your suffering's nothing to mine. Despised, rejected, laughed at, I'm closer to Him than you. And I've got better legs.

(*To the encouragement of the other clowns he puts on his red nose and hits himself with a slapstick.* PELLICO *and* LEFRANC *stop jerking about.*)

PELLICO: *Huhh, huhh,* buttock and twang! Can't do it. Me rhythm's gone.

LEFRANC: It's these rut-watchers, *huhh huhh.* I've lost the beat too.

(FLOTE *repeatedly hits himself with the slapstick and moves convulsively.*)

GREZ: (*Stabbing himself with increasing fury*) Become all fire this Easter, God's purifying flame. Beaten, tortured, saved! (*He slashes his throat by mistake.*) Uuuuugggg?

FLOTE: Devour my pride since it's devouring me. Transform me into Christ's substance, give me as food for the afflicted. (SONNERIE *slaps a custard pie in his face and he jerks violently.*) Aa-ooh-aah, let me be witless since Thou, Lord, art God and I am nothing. Use me, *aaa-ooh-aah.*

GREZ: (*Staggering*) Uuuuugggg.

FLOTE: (*Jerking*) Aaa-ooh-aah.

LEFRANC: *Aaa-ooh-aah?* Did you say *aaa-ooh-aah?* That's good. (*He imitates* FLOTE, *jerking violently up and down.* PELLICO *copies him.*)

PELLICO: *Aaa-ooh-aah,* we've got a good rhythm here.

LEFRANC: *Aaa-ooh-aah*'s the carnal beat, my bawds.

(PELLICO *and* LEFRANC *repeat* FLOTE's *jerkings exactly with* CAMILLE *and* MARIE *clinging desperately to their backs.*)

PELLICO: *Aaa-ooh-aah*'s strong stuff.

LEFRANC: Our thanks, Father, the square is yours for Easter!

PELLICO: *Aaa-ooh-aah.*

(*The* FLOTTIES *cheer and one by one pick up* LEFRANC's *and* PELLICO's *rhythm. As the two* GOLDMERCHANTS *exit Upstage Centre with* CAMILLE *and* MARIE *pushing the pile of gold,* FLOTE, TOULON, ROCHFORT *and* BRODIN *follow on behind in a line. Despite themselves,* GREZ *and the* FLAGELLANTS *join in and they all exit in an all-jerking, all-spastic version of the Conga.*)

THREE

MARGUERITE: If you can't join in, orgies're about as interesting
as watching cabbages grow. I used to pig it thrillingly every
night with my Jacques, wild peacocks and rainbow-
coloured whales. It was all as easy as hawks fly and fish
leap. Of course I was very young then and knew what I was
doing. When we met I let him make the first move and he
did – filthy beast, the Lord be praised. I'd often say, 'Get
thee behind me, Satan' and those were the worst words . . .
When Jacques died of the hot sweat, I felt the Church
'tween my thighs misery-moaning and holding me. I
thought cold chastity would clean my bones, sober my
heart. Mistake. Dead, Jacques was more alive than the
living Christ. Mountains crumble, seasons pass and I grieve
for what is gone, staining the night with tears. How to cure
the sunlit years, Master Bells? Affairs of the heart – who
really knows? Sometimes I forgot to get up or straighten my
hair. My life became full of low ceilings, walls set at right-
angles. But with Father Flote's help I'll break 'em down
and soar. I've so much to give yet I beat my gums in the
wind. I'm a giantess who's hidden her life. I want to leave
my mark. (SONNERIE *rings his bells*.) 'Close your eyes,
Marguerite, and change horses.' So, so . . . there's no rage
in you like the rest of us, Master Bells. You're a gentle
gentleman, tell me about bells? (SONNERIE *jumps and
gestures, ringing his bells*.) Yes. Squilla. Nola. Kodon.
Krotalan. Cornguincula and Cymbalum. And the bells you
wear? All Tintinnabula . . . I see. What? Roman Emperors
hung bells on their triumphant chariots to remind them of
human misery and a bell guided Lazarus back into this
world from the dead. Why bells, Master Sonnerie?
(SONNERIE *takes out two handbells and rings them softly. He
stops, then rings them again with more emphasis*.) Your
children were dying. You shouted, 'Don't die, I love you all
so much' but they went on dying. So much love and no way

of defeating death. Perhaps the bells'll bring them back like Lazarus . . . Ah . . . Teach me the language of bells, Master B. (SONNERIE *gives her a handbell; he rings his and she replies with increasing confidence.*) Straight ring, back ring, roll, semi-roll, swing. I hear the passage of time. You're the only sane man in this brain-bald world, Master B. (*He changes his handbell from one hand to the other; she laughs.*) And I'm. . . ? What? Tender as an oriole, matchless as the sea, hidden starlight, moonglow, enough sunshaft in my hair to burn another Troy . . . You've the true gift of tongues, Master B. (*He rings his bells.*) 'Bid me live and I will live . . .' (*She replies by ringing.*) 'A loving heart to thee . . .' (*She rings.*) 'A heart as soft, a heart as kind . . .' (*She rings.*) 'That heart I'll give to thee.'
(*They dance together accompanied by their bells and the butterflies, which gently beat their wings in time to the song. It ends and the butterflies are taken up.*)

FOUR

BRODIN *and* ROCHFORT *enter Upstage Centre in monk's habits,*
pulling a small, half-painted, portable stage. It is large enough for
two actors, with steps up either side and a primitive curtain.
SONNERIE *assists* BRODIN *painting the stage and* MARGUERITE
helps ROCHFORT *with two masks.* ROCHFORT *puts the comic mask*
in front of his face.

ROCHFORT: People are dying this year who've never died
    before. Princess Joan, the daughter of the English Edward's
    been taken plague-sick on her way to marry Pedro of
    Castille. I used to have a sneering acquaintance with Pedro.
    (*He gives* MARGUERITE *the masks to hang on the side of the*
    stage, then lies back, yawning.)
MARGUERITE: I'll toss a coin, Brother Rochfort. If it lands on
    its edge you start working.
ROCHFORT: Sister, there're three classes: nobles who do the
    enjoying, clergy the praying, and the rest the working. I
    belong to the first class but am forced to travel third. We
    were rich. My family never wanted for anything. Except
    Cousin Pierre, who's wanted for rape and murder. But I
    had no portion in my father's inheritance and no other
    calling but arms. Bastards are given no caps for their heads
    when they take to the road. When I left nobody noticed I'd
    gone. But they'll notice when I return. Oh, they'll be a fine
    noticing when I return.
MARGUERITE: Anyone can see you were born a gentleman,
    you're so useless.
BRODIN: Genoese pikemen are now scouring the plains of
    Champagne for plunder; found only thorns and brambles,
    bitter bones, sick ghosts and ruined walls. They sent word
    for us to join 'em. I said it wasn't worth it till Master
    Pestilence is seen off and Mars reigns again. (*He slaps on red*
    paint.) Give us rest and peace the people cry. But rest in
    peace is for tombstones. Father Flote'll make people laugh

again, give 'em back the courage to kill and be killed.

ROCHFORT: Perhaps I shouldn't think of myself so much, though it is an interesting subject. I find it difficult to do the same thing twice, even once. War, women and drink are just a series of amusements to help me escape boredom. I shrug, nothing makes any difference. But Flote's different; perhaps he'll change it.

MARGUERITE: Yes, he's a man who puts on his shoes backwards and walks into himself.

(FLOTE *enters Stage Left, reading a Bible. Looking up he sees the portable stage and, without pausing, tap dances up the steps, across it and down the other side.*)

FLOTE: Isaiah – who had one eye higher than the other – chapter 51, verse 11: 'Oh thou afflicted, tossed with tempest and not comforted, behold I will lay these stones with fair colours . . .' So lay on the fair colours, Master Brodin.

(TOULON *enters Stage Right.*)

TOULON: Are you ready, Father? The new recruits are here. Every halfwit and quarterwit left breathing.

FLOTE: The bright-eyed and hopeful?

TOULON: The dull-eyed and hopeless. They come for free food and lodging not for love of God.

FLOTE: It's always Ash Wednesday with you, Father, never Easter. If they've skills, we need them in our troupe. The loving can come later.

TOULON: Let's judge them then.

FLOTE: Never judge, Brother Toulon. We're here to see if Christ can use them. Who's first?

TOULON: (*Reading from a list*) First is Jean Le Grue and Charles Bembo.

(*Shaking slightly with palsy,* BEMBO *enters Upstage Right carrying a canvas bag and a small drum strapped round his waist and accompanied by blind* LE GRUE, *furiously waving a white stick and hitting* TOULON *savagely with it as he passes him.*)

FLOTE: Are you Jean le Grue?

LE GRUE: (*Facing the wrong way*) No shafts, flashes, gleamings! Sunrise, sunset, shades of memory. Eyes like dead mussels swimming in gravy *ugh*. Why should you see and not me?

FLOTE: Could you tell us what you can do?

LE GRUE: Le Grue's the name, the great Le Grue. You've heard of me? Speak up, damn you, can't you see I'm blind? Take out their eyes Lord, as mine were took.

FLOTE: It would be best if you started.

LE GRUE: Do? I juggle. I'm the best stone-blind juggler in the French and Norman lands. 'Tis said Father Flote and his God-mad hoddy-doddies will feed us? Time's wasting, best get started, Bembo. (BEMBO *takes three clay plates from the bag, stumbles across and shakily hands them to him;* LE GRUE *gestures confidently and* BEMBO *plays a drumroll*.) I've got dead peepers, so all's done with my feather touch – better than live eyes. (*He throws the plates up one by one: one by one he misses them and they fall and smash to pieces on the ground, but he continues to smile confidently and juggle the empty air*.) I juggle so fast I can't feel 'em. It's one advantage of being blind, other senses're sharpened, *a-haa*. Watch the hands! The hands! (*He mimes throwing one plate higher than the others and passes another between his legs*.) Good, isn't it? Hi-up, Bembo.

(*He throws the imaginary plates to* BEMBO *who mimes catching them*.) You've never seen anything like that, eh? You admire now? There's more. The woods, Bembo! The woods!

(BEMBO *hands him three wooden clubs and plays another drumroll*. FLOTE *and the rest move back instinctively as* LE GRUE *throws the clubs into the air and misses them. They fall on his head and he slumps down with a groan*. BEMBO *picks up the clubs, bows to acknowledge the non-existent applause and drags off the unconscious* LE GRUE, *Stage Left*. SONNERIE *rings his bells, dazed*.)

MARGUERITE: Le Grue must be to juggling what Attila the Hun is to needlework.

BRODIN: If I'm not back by Wednesday, break down the door and let me out.

TOULON: (*Reading*) Pierre Frapper – quick wit and stand-up jibster, singer of songs and sender of frolics. Pierre 'Isuffered-for-my-art-now-it's-your-turn' Frapper.

(FRAPPER *enters Stage Right.*)

FRAPPER: S–s–s–s–sires a f–f–f–funny thing h–h–h–h–
er–er–t–t–t m–m–m on the w–w–w–ay but I c–c–c–can't
r–r–remember w–w–w–'twas. I–I–I–I m–m–m–ay be
slow b–b–but m–m–my act is s–s–sloppy. E–e–e–e–
r–r–r . . .

(BRODIN *guides him out Stage Left and returns.*)

ROCHFORT: Someone should throw a shoe at him and forget to
take out their foot.

TOULON: (*Reading*) Alain and Jacques Boutros. The Boutros
Brothers!

(*The* BOUTROS BROTHERS *enter Stage Right on crutches to
the tune of 'When you're smiling', thumping down on their one
good leg as they dance across the stage and exit Stage Left.*)

BRODIN: Don't panic.

TOULON: Did you ever see such Satanic pride? Pull it down,
thou art cut worms under the spade. That blind wretch
acting as if he could see, the dumb one speak, the one-
legged dance. It's God's judgement that the blind, dumb
and crippled stay so, till prayer and repentance change it.
They're guilty and must accept their punishments, not
make light of them in their vaunting pride.

FLOTE: It wasn't pride but hope, hope shining anew despite of
every discouragement. Brother Toulon, we just saw the
very apotheosis of Christianity: the triumph of hope over
experience.

TOULON: A definition the Supreme Pontiff will be most
interested to hear. (*He hands* FLOTE *a document.*) This just
arrived. The Holy Father, Pope Clement VI, commands
your attendance at his court in Avignon.

FLOTE: We must go to him immediately, if not before.

(SONNERIE *waves his arms.*)

MARGUERITE: Yes, my pigeon. Father, what of the Triple
Threat – Le Grue, Frapper and the Boutros Brothers?

FLOTE: They join us, of course. Did you not hear the laughter?
Failing to be good they succeeded in being completely bad.

BRODIN: They'd never make soldiers. I've got veins in my nose bigger than their arms. But such spirits raise the spirits. (*Chuckling*) Remember Blind John of Bohemia who fought with us at Crécy?

ROCHFORT: He faced the wrong way as well. Killed more of his own men than the enemy. (*Chuckling*) He was funny too, now I come to think of it.

MARGUERITE: (*Laughing*) Those plates, those plates!

FLOTE: (*Singing*) 'Let them join us. No weak link. Must keep trying. Else we sink. Join together just us few. Pierre Frapper and blind Le Grue. Charlie Bembo and the other two.'

TOULON: (*Singing*) 'Join together? Man's too frail. He's divided. It will fail. Join together not that crew. Pierre Frapper and blind Le Grue. Charlie Bembo and the other two.'

(LE GRUE, BEMBO, FRAPPER *and the* BOUTROS BROTHERS *enter Stage Left, singing.*)

ALL: 'Join together. That's the plan. It's no secret. Man helps man. Work together, make it new. Pierre Frapper and blind Le Grue. Charlie Bembo and the other two. Join together stick like glue. Pierre Frapper and blind Le Grue. Charlie Bembo and the other two.'

(*Lights out amid laughter and shouts of* 'Avignon! To Avignon!')

FIVE

Darkness. An owl hoots. An unseen animal slithers past. The sound of FLOTE *and the others singing 'Join together' in the distance. A lantern light appears Upstage Left, followed by a line of lights from eight more lanterns behind the first. It is* FLOTE *and his troupe. They slowly make their way across the stage with* LE GRUE *in the lead.*

FLOTE: Master Le Grue, I have a shrewd suspicion we're lost.

LE GRUE: Lost? How can we be lost? I'm blind, aren't I? It's night, isn't it? Night is mother's milk to me. I live in it – curse these stone eyes. My senses are sharpened in the dark. Even now I can feel the warm rays of the early morning sun coming up over my left shoulder.

ROCHFORT: That's my lantern, you loon.

FRAPPER: I–I–I–I–I–I . . .

FLOTE: Is everyone still here?

TOULON: I'm here but I wish I wasn't.

(SONNERIE *rings his bells.*)

BEMBO: Bembo's here.

FLOTE: Where are the Boutros Brothers?

BRODIN: I'm carrying Boutros One.

MARGUERITE: And I'm carrying Boutros Two.

BOUTROS TWO: Careful, Mistress, I've only got one leg – that makes me lop-sided.

LE GRUE: Save your breath, Master Boutros, there's no sympathy for cripples here.

FRAPPER: . . . th–th–th–th–think w–w–w–e–e . . .

(*The sound of slow wingbeats overhead.*)

MARGUERITE: What's that?

ROCHFORT: An owl, an auk. Could be an ostrich bird?

MARGUERITE: Ah, something touched my face.

BRODIN: I only ever killed those I could see. Didn't like doing it in the dark. Something shameful there.

FRAPPER: . . . a–a–a–are . . .

TOULON: Yes, Le Grue, where are we?

LE GRUE: On the road to Avignon. I can smell the lemon trees on my right and the cool wind from the mountains strokes my left cheek.

TOULON: You mean you don't know.

FLOTE: You must have faith, Father, in men as well as God.

LE GRUE: Faith. Tell him, Bembo, we've travelled this road a hundred times, there's firm ground under our feet and I *aaahh*.

(*There is a loud splash as* LE GRUE *falls into a stream. Shouts from the others.*)

LE GRUE: I'm blind, I can't swim in water!

FLOTE: Pull him out.

ROCHFORT: I have you, Le Grue. Steady.

(ROCHFORT *is heard pulling* LE GRUE *on to the bank.*)

BEMBO: There shouldn't be a stream there.

FRAPPER: . . . l–l–l–lost.

TOULON: Well said, Master Frapper. Short and to the point. Lost. Father Flote, you expect to save this whole decaying world and yet you can't get us from Auxerre to Avignon.

(*As they come Stage Left they see the ragged figure of* COUNT ETIENNE VASQUES *sitting stock still illuminated in half-light.*)

FLOTE: Friend, can you direct us?

VASQUES: Don't move muscle, eyelid, nostril, stay stock still; though ants bite, birds nest in my hair, mongrels piss up against me, I don't move. Move and you die. Plague worms attack anything that moves. I eat, drink, move my bowels only at night so they don't see me move. When I was scholar and arse-licker at the Papal Court I shot up the greasy pole, bowed, sneezed, carried out orders. Now the afflictions of the hour make the greatest sit on the ground and I'm tired of thinking. It's why I live like a rock, think like a tree, abandon my mind, observe the thought forms fading and the gaps between the thought forms and I know nothing not even whether I know or do not know, only knowing I don't move for if I move Death will see I move and I'll move no more.

(VASQUES *shuts his eyes and goes rigid as his light fades out.*)

FRAPPER: W–w–w–w–h–h. . . ?

BRODIN: I agree, Master Frapper.

ROCHFORT: Have you noticed how you meet a different class of people at night?

LE GRUE: Onward, onward! Up and under!

(*As they move across the dark stage another half-light comes up ahead of them to show* BIGOD, *a burly man in a woman's dress and wig, wiggling his hips provocatively. His face is thickly painted and his long black beard tied with ribbons.*)

BIGOD: Hello, sailors, I'm gorgeous, aren't I? Gorgeous, untamed and immortal. It's the feminine principle, female gender that survives. We women spin and weave, all day, every day, spinning and weaving the tapestry of life and death, threads appearing and disappearing; everything that is, comes from us. (*Putting his hands on his hips*) Do you like my dress? Dazzling, isn't it? And the colours won't run, at least not unless they see you. Women endure war, famine, drought, pestilence, childbirth, childdeath; clearing the cesspool of the ages we develop muscles. I saw it when I was Chief Magistrate of Auxerre. Had adultresses stoned and witches burnt and they were stronger than me. Men break, we women endure. It's proven twice as many men are plague-dying than women. This dress doubles my chances. If Death comes I'll give him the soft eye. You men are all alike, the earth shakes but I'm as steady as a three-legged pot. The Virgin Mary looks after us girls, she does, and Death will pass me by.

(*He rushes away into the darkness and his light quickly fades out as* SONNERIE *shakes his arms.*)

TOULON: You're right, Master Bells, their hearts tremble, the terrors of death have come upon them.

MARGUERITE: A man must really be frightened if he wants to live like a woman.

(*There is the sound of* BLACK RAVENS *harshly caw-caw-cawing, high above them in the dark. Their lanterns tremble.*)

BOUTROS ONE: Time we moved on.

BOUTROS TWO: Which way?

BEMBO: Any way, so long as it's forward.

LE GRUE: Watch me. Stay close. I always move forward despite my affliction.
(*Lanterns and brazier glow Downstage Right.*)
FLOTE: Lights. See, see there are warm, comforting lights down there.
LE GRUE: I can't see 'em.
BRODIN: Of course you can't, you're blind.
LE GRUE: Oh yes . . . well, you don't have to keep reminding me.
FLOTE: They'll know how far we are from Avignon.
ROCHFORT: 'Twill be safer if we take the long way down.
LE GRUE: No, no, I know a short cut . . .
TOULON: Ignore him.
FLOTE: A song to overcome night fears, friends.
FRAPPER: L–l–let's h–h–h–a–a 'S–s–sit a–a–amongst the L–l–l–l . . .'
(*They move off singing.*)
FLOTIES: 'Sit amongst the lilies. Play your silver spoons. Kidney beans and privies. Spindle on your looms . . .'
(*The line of the lanterns disappears Upstage Left and a spot comes up Downstage Right on a small cart overflowing with dummy corpses.* SABINE PATRIS *is on top of it, stripping the corpses and throwing down the clothes to her husband* HENRI PATRIS *and mother,* MOTHER METZ.)
SABINE: Eight of my sons buboed gone. The youngest first. Death plays no favourites. Burn boils in his groin and armpits, his body shaking under fever winds, drowning in his sweat. I prayed to God, 'Save my child, Lord' but it's hard labour making God human. Oh, my pretty fig boy. He came so still like dew in April falling on the grass. He'd've grown into a fine thief and cut-throat. Make his parents proud had he lived. My mother lives – you wormy dogmeat. (MOTHER METZ *cackles.*) The hairless stay upright, the young fall.
PATRIS: If our boys had lived, we wouldn't be working now nights as well as day. Everybody left breathing prospers 'cept us. Too poor even to live off the dead we live off the men who live off the dead – the Black Ravens *caw-caw* who

44

tell us to spit on the dead fat-bellies. Spit.

(*They ritually spit on the corpses.*)

SABINE: We spit but we still have to pay 'em for the privilege of pillaging what's left of their corpses. We didn't draw no prizes in the lucky bag of life, Henri. (*She suddenly points at* MOTHER METZ.) Thieving mould-warp! I saw her, she stole something from us. (PATRIS *punches* MOTHER METZ *and snatches a silver buckle from her.*) Knock out her teeth, it'll mean more food for us. Die, snot-dribbler, die!

MOTHER METZ: I'd rather kill myself than die. I'll die the day after you die. You won't know it burning in Hell. Oh, there's no hatred like a mother's hatred for her daughter – she keeps giving me mirrors. You try to kill me, axe, rope, mortal poisons, but I survive beaver-bright, my will is stronger, chitty-head.

(SABINE *is about to scramble down after* MOTHER METZ *when* FLOTE *and his troupe enter with lanterns Downstage Left, singing.*)

FLOTIES: 'Sit amongst the lilies. Play your silver spoons. Kidney beans and privies. Spindle on your looms.'

SABINE: They sing idiot, there's no sense to it. It's Lucifer, Prince of Nonsense and his demons!

FLOTE: No, it's Father Flote, Father Toulon and friends.

TOULON: They're no friends of mine.

(MARGUERITE *sinks exhausted with* BOUTROS TWO, *whilst* BRODIN *dumps* BOUTROS ONE *beside him.*)

BRODIN: Where are we?

PATRIS: The Municipal Burial Yard.

LE GRUE: You see, journey's end thanks to me. The Municipal Burial Yard, Avignon.

MOTHER METZ: The Municipal Burial Yard, Auxerre. This is Auxerre, laddie.

ROCHFORT: But that's where we started from!

LE GRUE: Absolutely, so we're not lost, are we?

TOULON: You eyeless oaf.

FLOTE: Le Grue, Le Grue.

LE GRUE: I warned you. It's a madness expecting me to show you the way to Avignon. I'm blind.

45

PATRIS: Avignon or Auxerre, death turns both places into the same no-place. But a blind man leading, there's something wrong here. I'm no fool.

FLOTE: But I am. Flote the Fool.

PATRIS: I've heard of you and your zanies. I've got some good bird impressions – I eat worms.

TOULON: Not tonight. Could you just put us on the right road to Avignon?

MOTHER METZ: You take the left fork out of Auxerre.

LE GRUE: I knew it!

PATRIS: We never help nobody. It doesn't pay. But we're corpse-collecting that way tonight. You can follow us.
(*As* SABINE *and* PATRIS *begin dragging the cart off, they start to sing the* Dies Irae.)

MARGUERITE: 'Day of Wrath'? That's a tune that sets spirits sinking fast.

SABINE: It's our favourite.

TOULON: Mine too.

FLOTE: It's the way it's being sung. Sing out with a joyful heart and oh the difference . . . (*Singing lightly*) 'Day of Wrath, O day of mourning, see fulfilled the prophet's warning . . .'
(*The others take up the new upbeat version of the Dies Irae as they disappear into the darkness, Stage Right, their lanterns bobbing jauntily in time with the singing.*)

SIX

A choir singing the Exultant caelum laudibus *drowns out the* Dies Irae. *Lights blaze in the ante-chamber of Pope Clement VI in the Palace of Popes, Avignon. There is a doorway Upstage Centre covered with a rich purple curtain of velvet emblazoned with the coat of arms of Clement VI. Papal banners hang either side. A loud fanfare of trumpets and* FLOTE *and his followers are led in by a* PAPAL HERALD *Downstage Left.*

HERALD: Bow heads, bow knees for you are in Avignon in the Palace of Popes, the beating heart of Mother Church. Bow heads, bow knees in obedience.
(FLOTE *and the others kneel downstage right.*)
FLOTE: Is this all you do, Master Herald?
HERALD: Yes, but I do it well, don't you think? Bow heads, bow knees for St Peter's Successor, Keeper of his Keys, Visible Head of the Universal Church, the Ultimate Earthly Judge of what is lawful and unlawful, Christ's Vicar on Earth, Summus Pontifex, Pontifex Maximus, His Holiness, Pope Clement VI.
(*A great fanfare and the purple curtain opens Upstage Centre. Behind it is a large magnifying mirror set at an angle to show the adjoining room where the white-robed* CLEMENT VI *sits between two burning braziers. He holds up his hand. The* FLOTIES *approach and kiss the ring on his forefinger in the mirror.* LE GRUE *misjudges the distance and cracks his forehead on the glass. He collapses with a groan.*)
CLEMENT VI: Eighty thousand florins I've just paid that thieving bitch Queen Joanna of Naples for Avignon. Eighty thousand florins for this pest hole. Fifteen hundred died here last week. That's flosey Avignon.
BRODIN: But it's easily defended, Holy Father.
CLEMENT VI: I'm glad to hear you say that, Master Brodin. You view it with a soldier's cold eye. Besides I need a permanent home in France, Rome isn't safe. (SONNERIE *shakes his left*

leg.) Who would want to kill me you ask, Master Bells? Who wouldn't? Unfortunately few are graced with your grace. (SONNERIE *shakes his arms.*) Too true, Master Bells, without power it is easier to be graceful.

FLOTE: Why do you lock yourself behind a mirror, Holy Father?

CLEMENT VI: I fear contagion so I sit till the pestilence passes.

FLOTE: And the fires, Holy Father?

TOULON: As a reminder of the fires to come, are they not, Holy Father?

CLEMENT VI: No, my physician de Chaulic said they would singe the wingy plague worms . . . I tried to obtain credit from your father last month, Master Rochfort. Too many Jews are being killed. I've no one left to borrow money from so I'm forced to depend on local lords – without success.

ROCHFORT: My father is so mean he never breathes out. He believes charity begins at home and should stay there.

CLEMENT VI: Sister Marguerite, they say all the Sisters of Mercy fled the convent but were caught dead; God's fine hand there. Only you survived. You must be a woman of singular virtue.

MARGUERITE: I am, Your Holiness. A strict penitent mumbler. Long fasts on short bread, that's how I've kept my figure. I drink spring water and sleep on nettles. It does wonders for the skin.

CLEMENT VI: And you are Pierre Frapper?

FRAPPER: Y–y–y–o–u–u–H–h–h . . .

CLEMENT VI: You must tell me a joke, when I have a week to spare. The Boutros Brothers – blessings on you. And Master Bembo and Le Grue.
(LE GRUE *has recovered.*)

LE GRUE: The Great Le Grue. There's only one, Your Holiness. Give him the teeth, Bembo and the whole personality.
(*As* BEMBO *and* LE GRUE *smile toothily,* CLEMENT VI *gestures for them to step back.*)

CLEMENT VI: Now I wish to speak with Fathers Toulon and Flote.

(*The others move away Stage Left and kneel.*)

TOULON: Your Holiness?

CLEMENT VI: These are hard times, my sons. The Church lies
gutted. I've no healthy clerics left for the important work of
collecting taxes and drafting new laws. Meanwhile kings
grow more powerful daily and nation states rise up to
challenge the Universal Church and I'm giving up hope for
Lent.

FLOTE: The Church is corrupted from within, Your Holiness.
The Shepherds of Christ fleece their flocks, buying livings
cheap and selling indulgences dear. There's no goodness
any more.

TOULON: I try to tell him, Holy Father, the corruption of the
Church is final proof of the strength of our faith. If the
Church were perfect there'd be no merit in obeying its
dictates. Make it more corrupt, Holy Father, more lustful,
usurious. The greater the Church's corruption, the greater
the test of our obedience. Christ lies in his grave but will
sprout up green above those clouds.

CLEMENT VI: No mysticism, Father Toulon, this isn't the place
for anything spiritual. Men've been corrupt since the Fall,
the wax drips into eyes and ears. Goodness is the real
danger, not corruption. Guard against the corruption of
goodness, Fathers. Who knows what will result from one
wild act of goodness. Charity makes destitution permanent.
To give everything you possess to a beggar is to kill a
consumer and put a hundred men out of work. A soft heart
is a millstone. Remember St Augustine's prayer, 'Make me
a good man, Lord, but not yet.' Don't be good, Fathers, be
right! And we can only be right with and by the Church,
for history has provided no other way of being right.

FLOTE: But where is God?

CLEMENT VI: Go ask a theologian. I'm only a Pope, elected by
French Cardinals, supported by a French King. And I'm
too busy trying to hold this world together as it breaks to
pieces. It's why I must have men about me who're better
than good, men who know when to fight and when to run,
when to make promises and when to break 'em. No action

49

too vile, no task too bloody. Give me wolves. Sheep I can
find. But where are the wolves who'll serve? (*He howls like
a wolf*.) *Arrwaaa*. Where are the wolves? *Arrwaaa*.

FLOTE: But wolves don't see the hurt man or hear the starving
child, the lark's summer song.

CLEMENT VI: It's a small price to pay to remove the terrible
necessity of choice from mankind. The people want bread
and certainty. But that's not for you, Father Flote. Do you
truly believe you can lighten the suffering of those who
aren't lucky, rich or clever enough with your red noses,
orange wigs and Easter Festivals? Are you and your Holy
Rollers of use to the Church?

FLOTE: When St Francis came before Innocent III, His
Holiness told him to caper in the dirt with pigs. St Francis
did so and God opened the Holy Father's eyes and Pope
Innocent blessed and sanctioned St Francis and his
Franciscan Order.

CLEMENT VI: I'd've sent St Francis away with a flea in his ear,
which he no doubt would've blessed – Brother Flea, Sister
Louse. Since the Franciscans have elected an anti-Pope and
have been burnt at the stake for heresy, they're not a good
example to follow, Father.'

TOULON: Flotism would encourage worse rebellion, Your
Holiness. Laughter produces freedom. It's against all
authority, ripping off the public mask to show the idiot face
beneath. When we're lifted to joy, we're taken out of the
world and glimpse the world as it could be. Only God can
be trusted to give us those delights.

FLOTE: I'm God's blind instrument, His obedient servant,
chosen to bring the salvation of joy to the fearful and pain-
racked.

CLEMENT VI: You talk of obedience. Will you disband your
Red-Nosed Brotherhood if I ask?

FLOTE: Holy Father, Holy Father, when I was born my father
said, 'Put him back, things are terrible enough as it is.' My
mother cried so much the ale ran out of her eyes. Don't
make me put out the light, spit on the spirit. God calls me
to open Hell's gate.

CLEMENT VI: And if I call you to forsake mirth, will you obey?

FLOTE: Holy Father, I twist in the wind, seared and shrivelled over five eternities.

CLEMENT VI: Will you believe I am His true voice on earth, Christ's voice, and obey?

FLOTE: Flesh breaks! I obey, *aaa-ooh-aah*. (*He jerks violently*.) Noses go down. I renounce mirth and joy.
(*He falls on his knees*.)

CLEMENT VI: You don't have to, Father. I summoned you to Avignon to bless your Red Noses. You are to be encouraged and financed by the Papacy. In time, draw up a Rule so the Floties can be recognized as a Religious Order. Now I order you up, Father, up.
(FLOTE *staggers to his feet as* TOULON *sinks*.)

TOULON: No 'tis a mistake, Holy Father.

CLEMENT VI: And you're it. Living behind a mirror, I look out and see there's liberation in the plague air as well as worms. The restraints, customs and laws of centuries buckle, the old moulds crack – happen they should crack – but the green force that liberates the poet and thinker also frees the maniac with a butcher's knife. The way's rough; no level roads left. I see you as a useful lubricant, Father; holy oil.

TOULON: No. He's grit in the wheel. This man sins, Holy Father. What would you call a priest found consorting with a lusting, wanton nun?

CLEMENT VI: Lucky. No more tit-knackeries, Father T. The Church is endangered. My liver turns hard as rock and I'm snared in the web of the world. New enemies call for new methods to combat 'em. Go out, Father F, give 'em joy this Easter. Dazzle 'em and take what's left of their minds off the harsh facts of existence. Ripple and spread!

TOULON: Bright dew turns to frost; lies run down the walls. I cannot look on your face, Holy Father.

CLEMENT VI: Go out in the name of the Lord. Ripple and spread, Floties!

FLOTE: Ripple and spread!
(FLOTE *and* TOULON *join the others who leap up and throw confetti over themselves in delight*. CLEMENT VI *makes the sign*

51

of the cross over them and they are all ushered out by the
HERALD, *Downstage Left, as lights go down to a spot on*
CLEMENT VI.)

CLEMENT VI: I'll pray. Lord, protect those who're still heroic
and loving, not seeing the futility of being heroic and
loving. Protect Father Flote; let him remain a blind
instrument. Don't open his eyes as mine were opened.
When I was young, I was a holy vaulter too. I had wings
and a full head of hair. Every year I competed with the
spring. But there's been a drying out. Heart's not the same.
I've used up all my bright gold. A life which can't answer
the question, 'Why live?' isn't one. (*A distant choir sings the
plainsong* Te lucis ante terminum.) Despair without bottom,
distrust so deep you distrust your distrust. Misery without
meaning. Soul's hinges rust. (*Singing*) 'And that's just fine.
I mean, it's fine that all things fade. And when they write
about these times. A hundred years of war and plague will
get one line. And that will do. If they recall these days of
death. They'll be asking Clement who? They won't care or
even try to guess what men went through. And that's fine
too. Because I've work to do . . .' And stop that pestilential
howling. You call it singing, I call it neuralgia. Curtain!
(*The curtain falls across the mirror. Spot out. The plainsong
fades.*)

52

Easter bells ring out joyfully as lights up on bare main square of Auxerre. BRODIN *and* FRAPPER *drag in the freshly completed small portable stage Upstage Centre, followed by* FLOTE *and* TOULON *rehearsing their parts in the coming playlet. The portable stage is placed Downstage Left. As* TOULON *gestures grandly and* FLOTE *corrects him,* MARGUERITE *enters Stage Right helping* SONNERIE *put on a bonnet and bib.* ROCHFORT *enters Downstage Right with* LE GRUE *and* BEMBO.

ROCHFORT: Father Flote, surely my part in this Easter play of
    yours is too small, considering I'm one of the few here who
    can read?
FLOTE: Later, Brother Rochfort, later.
    (*He exits hurriedly Stage Left with* FRAPPER.)
FRAPPER: M–m–my p–p–part is v–v–v–very v–v–v–very
    –l–l–long.
ROCHFORT: You're lucky. I've only some five lines to say.
FRAPPER: I–I–I've only g–g–g–g–got one.
LE GRUE: What're you complaining about, Rochfort? I've got
    no lines at all. I stay dumb.
TOULON: That will be the day, oh Lord.
    (*He exits Stage Left.*)
LE GRUE: And Bembo, Bembo doesn't say anything either.
BEMBO: I rarely do. I've no chance.
    (*He guides* LE GRUE *off Downstage Left as* SONNERIE *shakes
    his body.*)
MARGUERITE: Yes, I feel nervous too, lamb, like I did the first
    time I lost my virginity – I was always leaving it around
    though I've still got the box it came in. This is our first
    public performance. Will we be a success?
ROCHFORT: Never fear, sweet chuck, I'm sure you'll get a warm
    hand on your opening.
BRODIN: But what of the parts we've been given in this Easter
    play? Father Toulon playing God?

ROCHFORT: To call him wooden is an insult to trees.

MARGUERITE: I love his voice though except for two
things – my ears. And what of Master Frapper?

ROCHFORT: He doesn't stop a show, just slows it down a lot.

BRODIN: And Father Flote playing Death? It's obvious I should
be playing Death. I know about death. I'm not your
everyday Everyman.

(SONNERIE *jumps and shakes his legs.*)

ROCHFORT: You're right, Bells. It's up to us four to make this
entertainment a success. But I confess to beads of sweat I
haven't felt since I was at Court and the King actually
spoke to me.

MARGUERITE: What did he say?

ROCHFORT: 'Move over, crow-bait, you're standing in my
sunlight!'

BRODIN: Sweat? I can tell you about sweat. Before a battle I
used to sweat buckets. Ah, but afterwards . . .

MARGUERITE: Why, what did you do after a battle?

BRODIN: Bleed.

(*Church bells ring again.*)

MARGUERITE: It's time, red-nosey time. The audience is
coming!

(MARGUERITE, BRODIN, ROCHFORT, *and* SONNERIE *hurry
off Downstage Left. A bright banner with the words:* CHRIST'S
CLOWNS PRESENT THE PLAY – EVERYMAN *unfurls Upstage as*
PEASANTS *and* ARTISANS *enter Upstage Right and* SABINE
and PATRIS *pull on their small cart Upstage Left with*
MOTHER METZ *on top of it, keeping the sacking, which covers
the cart's contents, in place.*)

SABINE: Putrid prune! Smell-feast!

MOTHER METZ: Flaggy dustworm! Stinking mard!

SABINE: You're no mother of mine, funge-bucket. Don't just
stand there, Henri – throttle her. Why is she still living?

MOTHER METZ: Because I sleep with my eyes open, scrat-face.
If you relax just once death slips in. I never relax. So I
breathe, *pa-pa-pa.*

(DRUCE *and* SCARRON *enter Upstage Left, cawing.*)

SCARRON: You sneaked away, Master Patris. The army of the

oppressed grows. Even the dead march with us. For they
know at least what it is to be poor, lying in cold dirt and
shadows, living out their deaths, as they lived out their
lives. The Emperor of Eternity who puts the damp in walls
and the white in old men's hair will be leading us, the Dark
Angel who tempted Eve out of that puerile garden and said,
no, to the status quo.

PATRIS: But all we did is come to see if there's any laughter in
the poor-house air.

SCARRON: There isn't and you don't need it. Stay hard, learn to
touch the very bottom, then the only way is up.
(MOTHER METZ *throws back a corner of the sacking on the
cart to show the corpses underneath.*)

MOTHER METZ: They don't know how, Master Scarron.
They're too soft to spit. But I spit. See, here's Dr
Antrechau and there's a forgotten Prince who once had cap
and knees of all men – now just things left behind.
(*She spits on them as* SCARRON *leaps up beside her.*)

SCARRON: My thanks, Mother. Remember the oppressed are
legion. And when all the holes in their belts are used up,
we'll destroy the soft hands, fat bellies and take their fine
places.

MOTHER METZ: Then will I have furs enough to cover the
moon? Wine enough to drown Jerusalem? Alps of
powdered sugar, stewed prunes and mutton for dinner?
Silk, worsted and fine yarn stockings, pockets in my goodly
robes so I can say, 'Give me the money 'cause I'm the only
one with pockets'? Will I have six petticoats and lace ruffs?
Will I be rich?

SCARRON: You'll be better than rich, you'll be of value. The
poor come truly rich when they give themselves value. Spit!
(*He and* MOTHER METZ *start to spit on the corpses as* MARIE,
CAMILLE, PELLICO *and* LEFRANC *enter Upstage Centre and
cross Upstage Right.* DRUCE *hastily covers the corpses on the
cart.*)

DRUCE: Scarron, you're making an exhibition of yourself. I'm
embarrassed, there are ladies present. We're in enough bad
odour as it is.

55

MOTHER METZ: That's the corpses. They can stink something awful. No one listens to freedom's call, Master Scarron. I tell 'em the bread's crucified, the onion weeps, the paper's ground to dust and they don't listen.

SABINE: Your brains are wet straw. Die, damn you, die!

(*As* MOTHER METZ *cackles,* LE GRUE *bustles in Upstage Centre waving the people into their places with his stick whilst* BEMBO *adjusts the small drum strapped to his waist.*)

LE GRUE: Spread out, you clodpoles. This way, follow me. You go there. No, you . . . dummy. This is the best position to see everything. (*He has his back to the small stage.*) If you ahh . . . Bembo! (*He bumps into* CAMILLE *and feels her body with his hands, lingering over her bosom.*) Charles? Charles Bembo? (*He feels her face and kisses her.*) You're not Charlie Bembo! You can't fool me. (*He staggers away.*) Anyone who's plague-stricken during the performance, have the decency to die somewhere else. Don't spoil it for others. (*A loud whip-crack and* GREZ *and two* FLAGELLANTS *enter Upstage Centre.*)

GREZ: Whip-scarred, Cain-marked, my brother came to me in tears, dying. I appealed to God who pronounced His most terrible sentence – life! He was given a life sentence. So my wretched brother lives. That's just one of the stories you would have heard if the Flagellants had been given the square this Easter. Stories to purge you with the terror and the pity of it. But in dark times people want creamy bon-bons not solid fare, hard tack. So you'll be entertained, *ugg*.

LE GRUE: Try not spattering blood all over the place, Master Grez. Somebody has to clean it up. *Shhh*, the show, the show begins!

(*A trumpet sounds and* BEMBO *beats his drums and* FRAPPER *enters Upstage Centre with a proclamation. The* AUDIENCE *facing the portable stage, Downstage Left, settle down in anticipation.*)

FRAPPER: (*Reading*) O–o–o–o–o–o . . .

(BEMBO *gently takes the proclamation from him and reads.*)

BEMBO: Oyez, oyez. Give audience to our play. 'Tis called *Everyman* and fair or foul, it will include one short interval.

Mirth's our purpose, so smile. And if you like it, clap your hands the while. See the first scene's in Heaven, where God dwells. We thought you'd had too much of Hell.

(*The small stage curtain rises to show* TOULON *in a white robe, seated on a wooden throne against a blue backdrop. He puts on a paper crown and a white wig. All the performers have on their red noses.*)

TOULON: I'm God.

GREZ: It's a lie. I know that voice. He's not God. It's Father Toulon.

(BEMBO *shoos him to silence.*)

TOULON: I'm God! But all my creatures now live without dread of me. Blind to my power, forgetful I sent my son down, felt his thorns and split side. Who now gives thanks for my mercies? (BRODIN *enters in a smock Upstage Left and falls on his knees in front of the small stage.*) Ahh, my sweet favourite – it's Everyman. He has not forsaken me . . . (BRODIN *rolls a pair of dice.*) Ingrate, drowning in sin! You'll come to feel my anger. I summon Death.

(*Gasps from the* AUDIENCE *as* FLOTE *with a whitened face enters Upstage Right and goes on to the small stage.*)

SCARRON: Death? Another lie. That's your red-nosed sallow-pate, Flote. We Ravens know about death.

DRUCE: Where're the women, Scarron? I came here for the women.

(*On the small stage,* TOULON *beckons* FLOTE *to him.*)

TOULON: Death, see how they live without fear. Go visit Everyman in my name and take him on his last journey. No, wait, he prays.

BRODIN: (*Kneeling*) Lord God, only hear my prayer. I can never get a fire started. Could you make me a burning bush in my backyard?

TOULON: Oaf imperfect! Go Death, bring him to his reckoning.

FLOTE: Lord, I cut down the fairest flower at your command. But I must be suitably attired first.

TOULON: Put the fear of God back into him. Drag him off to judgement. Go down, Death!

(FLOTE *bows, the curtain on the small stage falls and*

57

MARGUERITE *enters Upstage Right with pot and dishes and crosses to* BRODIN, *followed by* SONNERIE, *dressed as a baby with a bonnet and bib, and holding a rattle.* MARGUERITE *puts down the pot and the others gather round as she ladles out porridge.*)

MARGUERITE: Did you pray for riches, Everyman? You promised me riches and everything that goes with it and all I got was everything that goes with it.

BRODIN: You can be very outspoken, my dear – but not by anybody I know. You make a happy man very old.

MARGUERITE: Remember how it rained at our wedding. Even nature wept.

BRODIN: Why don't you go for a walk in the woods and trample on the flowers? You'd like that. (SONNERIE *gurgles and flicks porridge at him.*) That's not my son. I've seen better specimens in glass jars. When you said you wanted to hear the patter of tiny feet, I told you to rent some mice. Oh misery, when the warm weather comes I'm going to drown myself. It can't get worse.

(*The curtain rises on the small stage behind them to show the white-faced* FLOTE *dressed in a long black cloak and gloves and carrying a scythe. The* AUDIENCE *gasps:* 'It's Death. Death's amongst us!' FLOTE *moves menacingly down the small stage steps, becomes entangled in his cloak and falls headlong with a cry.* BRODIN *and the others look round as* FLOTE *scrambles up.*)

FLOTE: Sorry, I was trying to make a good entrance. I like to sneak up on people . . . I used to think I was indecisive, but now I'm not so sure. You're wondering who I am? Guess . . . White face . . . black cloak . . . scythe . . . No? Prepare thyself, Everyman. I'm Death.

(SONNERIE *throws a spoonful of porridge in his face.*)

MARGUERITE: It's some stark pimp, a straw-in-the-hair moon-loon. And stop annoying my little boy.

BRODIN: You don't believe anybody. If he says he's Death, he's Death. He looks like Death. A face like that must've worn out at least two coffins. But I thought you'd be thinner.

FLOTE: (*Wiping his face*) Thinner? Me? There's not a spare gram of flesh on me. Thinner! Lookee, Everyman, God has sent me down to take you on a last journey. In His infinite wisdom He feels you've had it too easy. You aren't suffering enough so He sent me.

(GREZ *starts hitting himself in the audience.*)

GREZ: No one suffers enough, it's why we're plague-cursed! Only feel pain, the redemption of pain.

BRODIN: You'll feel the pain of my fist if you don't stop airing your gums.

FLOTE: No one disturbs your public whippings, so give our show a chance.

(*Shouts of agreement from the* AUDIENCE.)

MARIE: Let 'em play.

DRUCE: There's a lewd woman.

CAMILLE: Who's closed for the day, Master Wagtail. Padlocked.

PELLICO: And paid for.

BRODIN: To return to Everyman and Death. Thank you . . . I'm Everyman now . . . What do yer mean, God doesn't think I'm suffering enough? I'm married, aren't I? My wife's got a tongue that can clip a hedge. In the beginning she took to me like a duck to green peas. Now it's so quiet in bed I can hear ice melting.

FLOTE: I can't stay listening to you, Everyman. I'm a very important person.

BRODIN: You look terrible but you don't look important.

FLOTE: Depressing, isn't it? I didn't even enjoy getting to look like this. Everyman, prepare for the journey, *ahh.*

(SONNERIE *repeatedly hits him with his rattle.*)

MARGUERITE: You'd like to go, wouldn't you, Everyman? Anything to escape your responsibility. You'd up and leave me without a word. All you think of is your own enjoyment.

BRODIN: I'm not going because I want to, woman. I've no choice, have I, Death?

FLOTE: None.

MARGUERITE: Oh, you men always stick together.

BRODIN: Death, if I go, can I take a friend with me?

FLOTE: If you can find someone stupid enough. The more the merrier, *ahh*. That child is a monster, Madam.

MARGUERITE: It's true, we have to take him everywhere twice – once to apologize – but don't forget you're a guest in this house.

BRODIN: I'll ask Good Fellowship to come with me.
(ROCHFORT *enters Upstage Left, followed by* BEMBO, LE GRUE, FRAPPER *and the* BOUTROS BROTHERS, *all colourfully dressed.*)

ROCHFORT: Start the applause, Good Fellowship is here. That's me. Full of good fellowship and good sense. Like – 'A man who laughs when things go wrong has just that moment thought who he can blame it all on.'

FRAPPER: B–b–b–b–r–r–illiant, G–g–g–g . . .

BRODIN: Fellowship, Fellowship, I go on a hard journey, will you come with me?

ROCHFORT: I'll never forsake you, Everyman. We'll all come and lighten your steps thus.
BEMBO *whips out a notice with the word,* INTERVAL, *on it and then drums. The* BOUTROS BROTHERS *dance frantically,* LE GRUE *tries to balance a small box on his chin and juggle with two others and* FRAPPER *begins a joke,* 'A–a–a–f–f–f–funny th–th–thing . . .' *The* AUDIENCE *relaxes as* PEDLARS *enter, selling food, drinks and lucky charms during the interlude.*)

SCARRON: Rubbish. They haven't shown the world as it is or how we can change it.

PATRIS: It's a dead world, so how can we laugh?

SABINE: Scavengers can't laugh.

MOTHER METZ: Pedlar, have you got a magic pendant for my neck so my neck won't die?

DRUCE: Did you see Everyman's wife giving me the eye out there?

PELLICO: It all looks penny-pinched and tat-like to me. They should've spent more money on the whole thing – fields of gold, black velvet and damask lace. That always impresses.

CAMILLE: Death has good legs.

GREZ: No blood. If we Flagellants had been on show, you'd see blood.

(*The drumming stops. The* AUDIENCE *shushes* SCARRON *and* GREZ *to silence and the playlet continues.*)

BEMBO: Act Two. Everyman speaks.

BRODIN: Gramercy, Fellowship. Our journey's to the Last Judgement. This is Death. He's taking us.

ROCHFORT: Death? Did you say Death? *This* is Death. . . ? I thought you'd be thinner. Are you the Death that makes dead worlds and field mice stop breathing?

FLOTE: And I can throw a wet blanket the entire length of a room.

ROCHFORT: That changes the picture quite, Everyman. I recall pressing business elsewhere. Exit fast, lads. It's Death. D–E–A–T–H.

FRAPPER: D–d–d–eath? I–I–I thought h–h–he'd b–b–b–b thinner.

(ROCHFORT *and the others exit Upstage Right, all congratulating* FRAPPER *in actually getting out a line.*)

MARGUERITE: Tavern loafers! If they were a hobby they'd be collector's items.

FLOTE: Everyman, I want us gone. I've got others to attend to. Birds, trees, stones, distant stars are dying. I must be there. Say thy farewells, Everyman.

(SONNERIE *starts shaking his bells and* MARGUERITE *comforts him.* BRODIN *takes out his pair of dice.*)

BRODIN: A last game. Do you play dice, Death?

FLOTE: Does a cock crow? Is the Seine a river? Do I play? You've heard of dicing with death?

BRODIN: If I win give me an extra day of life. If I lose I come smiling.

FLOTE: I don't know if I should. I'd be taking an unfair advantage. You're obviously a simpleton. Tell me what is three plus three?

BRODIN: Nine.

FLOTE: Nearly. Only two out. Right, we'll play, Everyman. (*They kneel and* FLOTE *shakes the dice.*) Tut-and-whistle-show-some-gristle. (*He throws.*) Two fives.

BRODIN: (*Rolling the dice*) Two sixes. (*The* AUDIENCE *laughs.*) Shall we make it truly interesting and play for money as well, Death?

FLOTE: Two sixes. . . ? I don't carry money when I'm working.

BRODIN: You've accoutrements.

(MARGUERITE *feels* FLOTE's *cloak.*)

MARGUERITE: Poor stuff, look at the width of this hem.

FLOTE: This is insanity. You can never win, friend Everyman.

BRODIN: Well, my wife already thinks I'm mad because I like pancakes.

FLOTE: Nonsense. I like pancakes.

BRODIN: Oh good, would you like to see my collection? I've got hundreds.

FLOTE: All right. Throw the dice.

(*As they start to play again a sharp high-pitched sound stops them. They and the* AUDIENCE *turn to see* MOTHER METZ *shaking with laughter.*)

MOTHER METZ: Hundreds of pancakes . . . hundreds of pancakes . . . I see hundreds of pancakes . . . (*As her laughter grows louder she suddenly slumps down.*) I'm Mother Metz and earth is in my ears. I relaxed and dusty death's slipped in through the cracks. Oh God looks down and men look up, blind to life . . . Pancakes . . . I'm dying . . . *Heee-heee* . . . I mustn't laugh . . . If I stop laughing . . . *Heee-heee* . . . I'll live . . .

(*She dies.*)

SABINE: She's dead.

(*The* AUDIENCE *shrinks back.*)

PATRIS: (*Laughing*) Now that is funny. Here lies Mother Metz, who when her glass was spent, kicked up her heels and went.

SABINE: (*Laughing*) Poems and epitaphs are but stuff. She laughed and died . . .

SCARRON: That's enough! Don't laugh and blunt the cutting edge of hate.

DRUCE: *Shhh*, let's get rid of her quick. I want to see what happens next in the play.

(*Using his pole, he quickly hooks the body off Upstage Right.*)

CAMILLE: The play! The play!

(*The playlet continues and* FLOTE *resumes rattling the dice amid laughter.*)

FLOTE: Tut-and-whistle-show-some-gristle . . . (*He throws.*)
Curses. Four and three.

BRODIN: (*Throwing dice*) Two fives.

FLOTE: Your dice are as hollow as my head. Cheat, cheat!

BRODIN: It's a lie. I've nothing up my sleeve.

MARGUERITE: And very little down your pants. Your clothes, Master Death.

FLOTE: I've fallen into a nest of thieving daws, *ahh!*
(*Amid howls of laughter from the* AUDIENCE, SONNERIE *dumps a bowl of porridge on his head as* BRODIN *and* MARGUERITE *rip off his breeches.*)

BRODIN: What are those hairy things you're wearing?

FLOTE: Hairpants. They're more uncomfortable than the traditional hairshirt. Hands off me, Madam!

MARGUERITE: Cloak and jerkin.

BRODIN: Debt of honour, Death.

FLOTE: Save me!
(*As* MARGUERITE *tears off his cloak and jerkin,* TOULON *appears as God on the small stage behind them.*)

TOULON: I'm the Alpha and Omega, the Life, the Way, the Truth, and I can't boil an egg or get my commands carried out. Death!
(FLOTE *stands shivering in his hairpants.*)

FLOTE: Lord, why are you always watching? Don't you trust me? I'll win it back. It isn't my fault. I was doing my best.

TOULON: Your best? I told you I didn't want failure! What race have I bred up who can send back Death a bare-arsed beggar? You are reprieved, Everyman, for the days you won back. But Death will come again.

BRODIN: We'll not fear him, Lord. For he's proved a cogging cheat. Death doesn't count, and probably doesn't read or write either. When he comes again we'll play it to the very end. Whether dying in a privy or marble halls, green field or white bed, the hand pointing to zero, the smell in your throat, don't do Death's job for him. Don't start dying before you die, already half dead. Don't go easy, make him work for you, let the calendar tear its own leaves, fight dirty.

63

FLOTE: Ah, but after life's drudgery, when you are weary . . .?
BRODIN: That's the time to be merry.

> (BEMBO *plays the drum*, SONNERIE *rings his bells, as*
> ROCHFORT, *the* BOUTROS BROTHERS, LE GRUE *and*
> FRAPPER, *enter Upstage Right and Left. They jump,*
> *cartwheel and tumble, wave coloured ribbons, throw*
> *streamers and join* FLOTE *and the others as they come forward*
> *singing.*)

ALL: (*Singing*) 'No one complaining. No one disdaining. Their
loss or gaining. Your heart retaining. And goodness
remaining. And laughingly to agree. A chip and a cherry. A
dill and a derry. A trill on the berry. Whatever the devil
that may be. But lovingly to agree. Sleep well every night.
In living delight. And lovingly to agree. A chip and a
cherry. A dill and a derry. A trill on the berry. Whatever
the devil that may be. But lovingly, lovingly, lovingly to
agree . . .'

> (FLOTE *and* COMPANY *bow amid tremendous applause and*
> *shouts of approval from the* AUDIENCE, *which disperses Stage*
> *Left and Right, leaving* FLOTE *and the others laughing and*
> *congratulating each other on their triumph.*)

FLOTE: The Holy Father said ripple and spread. We'll ripple
and spread to every town and hamlet, village and dingly
dell. Spin, Brothers, spin. Spin and lose all sense of
direction let God guide you. Round, round, round!

> (FLOTE, MARGUERITE, ROCHFORT, FRAPPER, BEMBO,
> SONNERIE, LE GRUE *and the* BOUTROS BROTHERS *all*
> *spin.*)

MARGUERITE: We spin! And fall!

> (*They stagger and fall.*)

FLOTE: Now whichever way you are facing that's the way God
wants you to go to carry His glorious words of joy and bring
down the walls with laughter. Up, Brothers, up and exit
smiling!

> (*They get up and exit fast whichever way they happen to be*
> *facing. There are peals of laughter and applause Offstage at the*
> *various points they exited as the lights go down to the cries of*
> Floties! Floties! Floties!)

ONE

Lights up on the main square of Auxerre. A tired FLOTE,
ROCHFORT, TOULON, BRODIN *and* MARGUERITE *enter at
various points Stage Left and Right.*

FLOTE: We've rippled and spread, Brothers and Sister, these
long days. My body aches but my heart sings songs of
morning. We've given light to the dawn, stars to the night
and joyful motion to the dancing company that encircles the
Universe. Standing on tip-toe we struck our tents amid
stricken villages, roamed the unreaped cornfields and
showed them God and life triumphant.

MARGUERITE: (*Singing*) 'Everyday smiles we had. Though the
plague be sore and bad. No use crying, how sad, how sad.
We come to banish sorrow, banish fear. Smile, my dear, my
dear, my dear . . .' Six pregnant nuns bearing out their
bellies before 'em, joined me in singing that sweet song. It
was wondrous.

ROCHFORT: Unbeatable, unmissable, the highlight of the year,
they called my fluting in Chablis.

TOULON: In Vency, they said I was ludicrous. Ludicrous.

FLOTE: 'Beautifully' ludicrous, Father. There's a world of
difference there. It means they liked you. Our fame grows.
Now people come to us for comfort.

BRODIN: After every campaign, even the successful ones, it's
custom to tot up the butcher's bill – casualty check front
and centre! Bembo and Le Grue I saw an hour past.

ROCHFORT: The Boutros boys are safe.

TOULON: And I spied Frapper on the road earlier, telling a joke
to some villagers. He'd been at it four hours already so he
should be joining us later today.
(*There is the sound of bells.*)

FLOTE: And that's Master Bells, so all are accounted for, God
have mercy.

MARGUERITE: No, those are bitter bells, not our own

sweet Bells.

(*Instead of* SONNERIE, *three* LEPERS *shamble in Upstage Centre. Their faces and hands are completely wrapped in dirty bandages and leper bells hang round their necks.*)

FIRST LEPER: Lepers, lepers, unclean, unclean. Flesh, bone, speech, rot. The black pestilence shunssss ussss like the plague. There's no quick bursting burn boils for lepers. Men pay us to haunt houses. Our bodies rusty knives and sickles. Unclean, unclean. Make us laugh, Fathers, bring us joy. They accusssssse us and the Jews of starting the plague by poisoning the wellsss. We're dragged to fire-pitsssss pushed through eternity's doorss. Kingsss decree all lepersss be banished, Princesss of Provence set mobs to massacre ussss.

ROCHFORT: Scapegoats are needed. The poor are always destroyed, not because they're poor but because they're weak.

BRODIN: Hunting wouldn't be such fun for lords if the rabbits had swords. Cuirassiers, Brother Leper! Cuirassiers!

FIRST LEPER: *Sister* Leper. I'm Sister Leper! Fathers, clothe our sick bones with flesh, show us skies without blemish, clear mountains, ponds of silver, a sudden glimpse of Paradise.

FLOTE: It was easy for Christ, he only had to heal the sick, raise the dead, cleanse the leper. He didn't have to make them laugh, make them feel superior to someone worse off than themselves.

TOULON: Let me try, Father Flote.

FLOTE: The stage is yours, Brother T.

TOULON: William Raimbaut had a new sash. Fell into the fire and burnt to ash. Now the room is chilly. We haven't the heart to poke poor Willy.

FLOTE: Well told indeed, Brother Toulon.

(*As* FLOTE, BRODIN, ROCHFORT *and* MARGUERITE *enthusiastically applaud* TOULON *they turn and see there has been absolutely no reaction from the* LEPERS.)

FIRST LEPER: Despair deeper than that.

SECOND LEPER: We drown in the river of our tears.

66

THIRD LEPER: We walk into our deaths and leave only our
    silence behind us.
    (FLOTE *takes off his false nose, kisses the* FIRST LEPER *on the
    mouth and bows formally.*)
FLOTE: Madam, may I have this dance?
    (*He grasps the* FIRST LEPER *and they dance.* TOULON *and*
    BRODIN *take a* LEPER *each as a partner and dance too, whilst*
    ROCHFORT *plays his flute and* MARGUERITE *hums 'Red roses
    for a blue lady'.*)
FIRST LEPER: Balloons rise in us. For a moment I am daughter
    of the sun, glimpse mimosa trees, rainbow bridges, star
    flights.
    (*The dance ends. The* LEPERS *clap their hands in muffled
    applause.*)
SECOND LEPER: Now know what we're missing. We must take
    our share of such delightssss, come out of the shadowssss.
    Show the world who we are.
    (*She unwraps the bandages round her face to reveal nothing
    underneath except a rusty metal frame in the shape of a face.
    Suddenly there is the sound of a* CROWD *off, shouting,* Lepers!
    Lepers! Kill! Kill! *and a motley collection of* MEN *and*
    WOMEN, *carrying crossbows and black streamers on poles,
    surges in Upstage Centre. Before anyone can react they raise
    their crossbows at the huddled group of* LEPERS. *There is the
    sound of arrows in flight. The* LEPERS *are hit, stagger and fall
    dead. All is suddenly quiet, except for the distant 'cawing' of the
    approaching* BLACK RAVENS.*)
TOULON: Polluted sons of Balaam, this is private property!
    You're trespassing, spawn of Sodom.
FLOTE: You've shed innocent blood, friends, and birds have no
    trees to nest in.
    (FLOTE, TOULON *and* MARGUERITE *hold up their crucifixes,
    whilst* BRODIN *and* ROCHFORT *pull back their habits to show
    their swords. But the* CROWD *remains menacingly. As the two
    sides confront each other,* LE GRUE *enters with* BEMBO *Stage
    Left, holding a fistful of knives. All his fingers are bandaged.*)
LE GRUE: Where are you grubbers?! (*He stumbles against a dead*
    LEPER.) Asleep? Whilst you've been dormicing, Bembo

and me've been out working and practising. Yes,
practising. Though I'm the best I'm never satisfied. That's
the mark of a true artist. I've worked out this new bit of
juggling. With knives. Yes, knives. Watch. (*But the sight of*
LE GRUE *preparing to throw the knives is enough for the*
CROWD. *They back away hastily for the exit Upstage Centre.*)
Creeping away on tippy-toe, eh? I can hear your big feet,
I've got ears. No eyes but ears. Crump-backed thumpers.
You don't know what you're missing. An artist like me isn't
content with the old routines. This is all new stuff. New
and brilliant. Le Grue does it again. Wait! Wait!
(*He stumbles after them Upstage Centre.*)

FLOTE: Brothers, keep an eye on him, as his eyes are blinded.
(BRODIN, ROCHFORT *and* BEMBO *hurry after* LE GRUE *as*
FLOTE *looks down at the corpses.*) So I considered again all
the oppressions that're done under the sun. And beheld the
tears of such as were oppressed and they had no comfort.
(MARGUERITE *and* TOULON *exit sadly Upstage Right,*
FLOTE *kneels and prays as* SCARRON *and* DRUCE *enter Stage
Left, 'cawing' and singing.*)

SCARRON and DRUCE: (*Singing*) 'We are two ravens sat on a
tree. Down a down, hay down, hay down. We are two
ravens sat on a tree. We are as black as we can be.'

DRUCE: I knew there'd be garbage to collect. Butchered for
poisoning the wells, eh?
(*He hooks the corpses off Stage Right with his long pole.*)

SCARRON: If the wells were poisoned, we did it – the Black
Ravens. They know but they're too frightened to move
against us. Did you try to save 'em, Father? I could've
saved 'em. My *caw-caw* would've sent the butchers
running. What did you do, but make 'em laugh.

DRUCE: Are they still laughing as they rot in eternity, Father?

SCARRON: Don't pray to your God of joy and laughter, He's
shut up shop long since. Pray to the Butcher God who did
this fine work.

DRUCE: Pray, Father, pray.

FLOTE: (*Rising*) As a boy my father put me on a ledge and told
me to jump and he'd catch me. I jumped, he moved and I

fell on my head and he shouted, 'That'll teach you never to
trust anyone, not even your father.' But I trust, trusting
you, Lord, even when you took my wife Marie and my
three little ones. My home was blasted for a purpose.
Ordained, I followed and trusted Your light, Lord. I'll not
let it flicker now. For still it is a joy to come in skipping,
leaping and dancing like a mad fool and plucking folk's hair
and making them swear by God. Exit dancing Flote.
(*He dances off Upstage Centre as* GREZ *and the*
FLAGELLANTS *enter Stage Right, chanting,* 'Pain, pain, pain'
and collapse.)

GREZ: In Rheims, Troyes, Bruges our flayed brethren march in
chanting and the streets are lined ten deep. They attract
multitudes of men, we can't attract flies. Our sacrifices go
for nothing though our Brother here broke his leg for them.

SCARRON: How did he do that?

GREZ: Easy, I took a hammer and went bang. No one was
interested. We need new ways to hold the public's interest
and fetch 'em to salvation.

SCARRON: The people suffer enough, they've no need to watch
your suffering. They want no more bloodstained martyrs
for Christ.

GREZ: Stinkards, you travel through your lives in the bowels of
the world like Jonah in that stenchy fish. Cleanse yourself
of hate and pride.

SCARRON: Penance-dribbler!

GREZ: Toad-eater! . . . Ah, converts.
(PATRIS *and* SABINE *have entered Stage Left.*)

PATRIS: Gentles, could you help us?

GREZ: Ave Maria, we return to Christ's passion, *ahhhhh.* (*He
stabs himself.*) They that sow in tears shall reap in joy. (*He
clubs the other* FLAGELLANTS.) No mortification too great,
no penance too hard. Ask anything of us. Ask!

PATRIS: Do you know where Flote and his big Red Noses are
performing?

SABINE: We're off to see the funnies.
(GREZ *stops clubbing.*)

GREZ: The Devil is now let loose to end the world and you want to see that flyblown sot, Flote. Decadent strumpet!

PATRIS: We've had too much of misery.

SCARRON: That's the world they've made for you. Change it. Spit, grease and change it, *caw-caw*.

GREZ: No, repent; repent and change it. Time stops, the book closes. (*A trumpet note is heard off Upstage Centre.*) The Last Trumpet sounds for Last Judgement!
(*But the trumpet note turns to a merry 'toot-toot', followed by a drumroll and laughter of a crowd.*)

SABINE: It's the Floties! The Floties!
(GREZ *clubs the* FLAGELLANTS.)

GREZ: Stay! Stay for the salvation of blood! See me smash his other leg.

PATRIS: Old stuff. Laughter's the new thing. Suffering and revolution is too hard. We want dolphins and dancing mice.

DRUCE: I think I'll join you.
(*Laughing in anticipation,* SABINE, PATRIS *and* DRUCE *exit Upstage Centre.* GREZ *stops clubbing, leaving the injured* FLAGELLANTS *groaning on the ground.*)

GREZ: I could have sat at home by warm fires, drinking wine in bowls. I was tutor to King Philip and slept on silk. I forsook all that, to help people like that, yet I couldn't hold them. The fault is in me. I've been too gentle. (*The* FLAGELLANTS *groan.*) We've not been suffering enough, Brothers.

SCARRON: No, only here in France is your Brotherhood of the Cross rejected and we Black Ravens are left without support. It's Flote.

GREZ: Yes, he's a clever fool. I once asked him which was more important, the sun or the moon? And he said, 'The moon because it shines at night when we really need it but who needs the sun when it's already broad daylight?' I confess, I've always had a soft spot for Father Flote.

SCARRON: A peat bog in the northern Ardennes. I say we grease the Noses dead.

GREZ: We're pledged to commit no violence. I must try and persuade him to join our Brotherhood of Whip and Cudgel.

SCARRON: The way he flogs old jokes it should be easy.

GREZ: But if he doesn't see the light?

SCARRON: We snuff it out.

GREZ: Well, so it goes. So it goes. We who come to cleanse the world of foulness are befouled by you cawing swine-scratchers.

SCARRON: Dog-leeches, you befoul life by taking away man's liberty and giving it to heaven. But I don't care who we join forces with – integrity's for failures. Death to the Noses!

GREZ: Death to the Noses! Brothers, you look slovenly. Straighten up there, don't slouch. (*Chanting*) 'Pain, pain, pain. Our journey's done in holy name . . .'
(*He exits Stage Right, with* SCARRON. *The* FLAGELLANTS *drag themselves out after them, feebly chanting,* 'Pain, pain, pain'.)

TWO

FLOTE *enters Upstage Centre, carrying a large wooden Cross,*
followed by MARGUERITE *with a pile of washing in a basket. As he*
places the Cross upright, Upstage Centre, BRODIN *and* FRAPPER
enter Stage Left with a long trestle table and two benches, followed
by ROCHFORT *playing his flute. The table is placed diagonally*
Stage Left and the benches either side. BRODIN *sits and carves the*
wooden face of a puppet, whilst FRAPPER *watches intently.* FLOTE
exits and re-enters with SONNERIE, *Upstage Centre, with bowls and*
plates for the table as MARGUERITE *hangs up the newly-washed*
clothes on the Cross to dry.

MARGUERITE: When you're young the summers never end,
later you can't hold a day. I'm losing time washing the crut
from your holy underbreeches. I keep asking myself, is
monastic life separating me from God?

ROCHFORT: 'He pressed me, I stumbled. He pushed me, I
tumbled. He kissed me, I grumbled. But still we kissed on.'
I wrote it for you, Sister Marguerite, to go with the air you
love so well.

MARGUERITE: 'He pressed me, I stumbled . . .' How shall I
sing it?

ROCHFORT: Under an assumed name. Didn't we meet before
somewhere?

MARGUERITE: It's possible, I've been somewhere. 'He pushed
me, I stumbled.' My thanks, Brother R. I'll make you some
wine, I've got very big feet.

FRAPPER: I–I–I w–w–wish I–I–I could s–s–sing. But I–I–I've
g–g–got n–n–n–no sense of p–p–p–pitch.
(FLOTE *and* SONNERIE *start bringing in various dishes of food*
Stage Left.)

ROCHFORT: Brodin, you should've seen Sister Marguerite and
me in Chablis. All were dead in the manor house except for
one goose-girl in her mistress's gown, dancing in those long
forsaken halls. I calmed her with playing my flute.

MARGUERITE: He proved a very perfect gentle knight.

ROCHFORT: My brother was dubbed a true one, invested in the robes, arms and the spurs of knighthood.

BRODIN: Hypocrites all. The horses've more breeding than the knights who ride 'em. Give me a fearful man-at-arms who knows when to run, not your glory-bound knight. (*He finishes carving.*) These hands have stabbed, slashed and clubbed fair flesh into two groats' worth of dead meat. Yet these hands are delicate enough to carve a doll's head and carry a fart to a privy. (*He gives the puppet to* FRAPPER.) Here, it's yours, Brother.

FRAPPER: M–m–m–much th–th–thanks, B–B–B–Brother B–B–B–Brodin.

(*There is a horrified cry as* TOULON, *who has just entered Upstage Centre, looks up at the washing on the Cross.*)

TOULON: Knickers? Fouled knickers and lace-edged underpants on the sacred sign of Christ's Passion! Christ's triumphant Cross bedecked with pogy undergarments.

FLOTE: Those pogy undergarments are but symbols of our devotion, Brother. Newly cleansed of body's corruption, they are offered up like our cleansed souls to God.

TOULON: Your tongue's boneless excusing every lace sacrilege. I don't see my hairshirt. Where's my hairshirt?

MARGUERITE: Burnt. It was rotted with lice and dead blood.

TOULON: I was attached to that hairshirt, Sister Marguerite. I had it with me man and boy.

MARGUERITE: We'll buy you a new one for Christmas, stuffed with holly. I thought we'd eat out here, Father Flote, as it's the last day of summer.

(LE GRUE *lurches in with* BEMBO *Stage Right.*)

LE GRUE: Snouts in the trough, trotters in the swill. Hog-hog-hogging without us, eh? I told you I smelt roast pork and neat's tongues, Bembo. No eyes but I've got a nose.

BEMBO: You've got that.

FLOTE: What've you been doing, Brother G.?

LE GRUE: Practising, what else? It takes practice to reach the standard I've set myself. I'm the Great Le Grue after all.

They expect something special when I'm out there juggling.
Where's the food?

FLOTE: Yes, let's pray and eat. We won't wait for the Boutros
Brothers. They've gone to see their wives in Volgre.

ROCHFORT: Actually they live in St-Cyr but they look better from
Volgre.

(ALL *rise*.)

FLOTE: Lord, as this bread upon the table was in separate grains
and being gathered together became one good thing, so let all
men and women be gathered together from the ends of the
earth into one family. In the name of the Father, Son and Holy
Ghost. Amen.

(*He makes the sign of the cross. They sit, and with* FLOTE *at the
head of the table, immediately attack the food, laughing and
talking loudly.* FRAPPER *tries to manipulate the puppet*.)

LE GRUE: (*Piling food on his plate*) Sot-faces, which of you's
snaffled my lace-edged underpants? That's stealing from a
blind man!

MARGUERITE: Can't you see I've washed 'em for you? Do you like
Brother Rochfort's special basted pike with crayfish sauce?

BRODIN: I'm for deep pots, wide pans, not mimsy portions served
in separate dishes.

TOULON: Ah, what food these morsels be. But we should only care
for the spirit, not meat and drink – pass the truffled capon *à la
moelle*.

MARGUERITE: Don't eat so fast, Le Grue. It's the first time I've
seen anyone get sparks from a spoon.

FLOTE: Pity there's no white wine. White wine's the most suitable
for poultry, if you can get 'em to drink it that is.

TOULON: The people of Vency gave Father Flote three chickens
gratis for being such a selfless benefactor of old jokes like that,
which had nowhere else to go.

ROCHFORT: Look, this chicken's got one leg shorter than the
other.

TOULON: Are you going to eat it or dance with it?

ROCHFORT: Time was I used to dine on godwits and pheasants,
snipes in osmagone sauce, boars' heads, rabbit fritters and
iced eggs.

MARGUERITE: The night before he died, my father sat up eating rabbit fritters.

BRODIN: Mine was badly murdered robbing a church.

TOULON: I was adopted, which is almost as good as being real. Jesu, there's a black thing with legs swimming in my soup.

FLOTE: What did you expect him to do, Father, lay there and drown? Come, let's help him out or at least stop him making waves.

LE GRUE: (*Blindly taking food from* BEMBO's *plate*) Neats' tongues! Why aren't there neats' tongues and frumenty? (*He stabs at* BEMBO *as he tries to take the food back.*) Hog off. That's a blind man's food you're stealing.

FLOTE: How went the day, Brothers and Sister? Master Bells, you always have a good tale to tell.

(SONNERIE *rings his right and left arm and then shakes his body, and his right leg. All lean forward listening intently whilst still eating. Reaching the climax of his story,* SONNERIE *leaps up shaking arms and legs simultaneously. The others bang the table in approval.*)

BRODIN: Marvellously well told.

TOULON: It will be hard to better that.

FLOTE: Father Toulon and me visited the plaguey houses of Vency.

TOULON: I told the dying there they should wrap themselves in their shrouds and walk to the cemetery. But *very* slowly so's not to start a panic.

FLOTE: He told it well, believe me.

TOULON: Yes, I think it had a certain style. Pass the pepper sauce.

MARGUERITE: Brother Rochfort and me knocked them stiff in Chablis – stiffer than they already were that is. Sometimes the soul lays hold of a voice and makes it sing what the soul has experienced and the voice doesn't know what it does. It happened to me in Chablis. I sang melodies I'd never heard before and I didn't know what I sang or how.

BRODIN: Then I joined them and we had a great success in Cheyenne. We was lucky. Their tax gatherer, old Gentile Bardi – the one with the money-bags under his eyes – hung

75

himself just before we arrived. It got us off to a swinging start.

ROCHFORT: Trying to get money from him was like trying to get dawn past a rooster.

TOULON: Money flowed out of him like drops of blood.

BRODIN: Is this wild rice?

MARGUERITE: No, tame, but you can mix it around if you like and make it mad.

LE GRUE: Applause. I'm deafish but I can always hear applause. It washed over us like the great sea. Not enough of course. It never is enough. Not for what we was giving 'em. We was brilliant. (*Leaning over* BEMBO) Wasn't we brilliant, Bembo?

BEMBO: (*Protecting his plate*) Passable.

FLOTE: What do you say, Brother Frapper?

FRAPPER: (*Finally manipulating the puppet's head and mouth*) The seething sea ceaseth seething . . . (*They all stop talking.*) Is there a pleasant peasant present? That's a three-twisted twist. Oh, list, list. Poor stuttering Pierre here prevented me before; always talking with his mouth like he'd swallowed a set of spoons but I'm in fine spoon fettle now. I tolerated him because he's an example of my kind of stupidity. I've words now, a whole world of words. In the beginning was the word and the end too. Words raise a wordy man above brute beast. Oh, my dame hath a lame crane. Pray gentle Jane, let my dame's lame crane home again. Come, stuttering Pierre, we'll share a single cedar shingle and certainly let my dame's lame crane home again.

(*All get up and crowd round* FRAPPER *with applause and congratulations.*)

LE GRUE: I've got ears. That's a new voice.

FRAPPER: An old voice, new found. Oh Brothers, oh Sisters, it's always easy to find fine friends to feel sorry for you but it's rare to find ones who will be happy because you're happy. My heart explodes in star-born whorls. The serpent spoke to Eve, cats and dogs to witches and warlocks, even echoes, without mouths, articulate and return the voices of

76

men in concave caves and hollow places. But I couldn't speak. Now my once broken words are the soaring wings of my soul, lifting me up to joy so I cease to grieve, to rage unspoken. I've whole words now so let the loud earth be at peace, let the upper air, hurricanes and tumults be still and the onslaughts of curling waves, mouths of mighty rivers and outswelling springs fade down, so my brightly blessed words, words, words can burst, burst, burst above you.

LE GRUE: No, that's not Brother Frapper.

FRAPPER: But I know behind the words are other words inaudible, and behind those words, there is silence. We don't fear it, thanks to you, Father Flote. You've made this another garden in Eden, opened Heaven so we can hear the angels sing, see the light that never darkens, made the mountains dance like rams and the hills leap like kids, blown away the miseries of the world as the wind does chaff and stubble so the sky is serene and fair again and the lands as rich as they ever were. In a word, Father, amongst so many words, you've made our hearts beat faster.

LE GRUE: No, that's not you. You can't fool Le Grue. I'm blind but I've got second sight. I spy strangers.

SCARRON: Too true, Le Grue!

GREZ: You do!

(*They turn and see* SCARRON *and* DRUCE *and* GREZ *and his* FLAGELLANTS *have entered silently Stage Right.*)

FLOTE: Welcome Brothers, there's food left.

SCARRON: Flote, you can't see the writing on the wall because your back's up against it. I'm greasing you!

(*Before anyone can stop him, he steps forward and breathes straight into* FLOTE's *face.* DRUCE *'caws' in triumph but* FLOTE *just stands there.*)

DRUCE: But they always fall when you breathe hard on 'em, Scarron.

(*Puzzled,* SCARRON *puts his hand in front of his mouth and breathes hard to test his own breath; he staggers back, shuddering.*)

FLOTE: I've kissed the leper, sucked in the wormy air of a hundred plaguey houses. Your breath's too weak to grease me out, Brother Scarron.

GREZ: Brethren of the Cross, it's time to inflict pain on others. Club down this grinning Anti-Christ. If you've a best foot left, put it forward!

(*As the* FLAGELLANTS *start to move,* BRODIN *and* ROCHFORT *pull back their habits to reveal their swords. The* FLAGELLANTS *stop.*)

BRODIN: Move anything and we lop it off.

GREZ: Defending yourselves, eh? I might've guessed you'd be up to such low tricks. Father Toulon, join us and suffer.

TOULON: Suffer? You don't know the meaning of true suffering till you've made a red-nosed idiot of yourself daily.

GREZ: You're not of this company, Toulon, join us.

TOULON: No, you're too selfish for me.

GREZ: Selfish? How can we be selfish? We have nothing.

TOULON: Then why do you act as if you have something?

GREZ: What, what, what?

TOULON: Your bodies. You punish your bodies as if they're yours. They're not; bodies belong to God.

MARGUERITE: Are you twiddle-poops eating with us or just standing around like a row of knackered Jack Puddings?

(SCARRON *stops testing his breath.*)

SCARRON: Chaos and death! Black Ravens, *caw-caw-caw.*

FLOTE: Sheath your swords. It's no time for killing, Master Pestilence needs no help from us. We'll judge who wins, who loses, who stays, who goes, by signs not swords. We'll appeal to Heaven. Let Heaven decide.

(*They all look up.*)

SCARRON: *Caw-caw-caw.* You up there, hear me, I sing the tender song of homicide. There's no Heaven or Hell but if a man has good fortune and lives well, that's Heaven, and if he lives poor and miserable that's Hell and he dies like a dog. Poor dogs are right in whatsoever they do to break out of ignorance and want. Hear me, hear me.

GREZ: *Ahh-ahh-ahh.* Hear me, Lord, I sing pain's song for Adam cast out of Paradise and the blood of Cain's brother crying to us out of the earth. Christ foresaw our falls, paid he not the price? War, strife, drunkenness, murder, we fall sore, we suffer sore. By suffering and obeying the God in their hearts men find their true strength and His favour the very seal and sign of an election in Christ before the beginning of the world. Hear me, hear me.

FLOTE: *Aa-ooh-aah*. Lord, hear me, I sing joy's song, green sunsets, purple mornings and crested coots. They asked, 'Why do you laugh while I am crying?' I answered, 'Because you are crying while I am laughing.' Life is given to us to be lived. God thunders, 'Marcel, you are still a fool.' I didn't see. Oh but now I see God shining, shining in glory. And I must tell you for a start – She's Black . . . Before our jibes lacked salt. But every jest should be a small revolution. We come to ding down dignity and make a new world, opening the gates of Paradise above and here below. Hear me, hear me. Only give us a sign, Lord.

(*Silence. Then a faint rapping sound. It grows louder and more frenzied as finally the* BOUTROS BROTHERS *hop in frantically, Upstage Centre, rapping their crutches on the ground to attract attention.*)

BOUTROS ONE: The plague! The plague is over!

TOULON: Over? Over where?

BOUTROS TWO: Everywhere! The cities of Paris, Villiers and Melun are clean.

LE GRUE: Why wasn't I told?

BOUTROS ONE: Rejoice. The Black Death ends and we live.

(*Stunned silence.*)

MARGUERITE: Live?

BRODIN: Live.

FRAPPER: Live!

(*Suddenly shouting and dancing, the* FLOTIES, FLAGELLANTS *and* BLACK RAVENS *find themselves hugging each other in a spontaneous explosion of joy.*)

FLOTE: It's the sign! God's sign we asked for. Explode the heart; air melt with joy. Deck yourselves with banners and with flags. It's time to cast off old ways, old thoughts. The old brown leaves are falling. Confronting death daily made us defiant, not humble, joyful not sad, sunflowers crazy with the sun. Blow trumpets for a new age, new world, light, birth. Master Scarron, Master Grez, we three are in the Millennium business and it's a waste to fight amongst ourselves. All forms of rebellion must come together. (*Singing*) 'Join together, that's the plan. It's the secret. Man helps man. Join together, that's the stuff. Black Jack Scarron in you we trust. Battered Grez and the rest of us.'

GREZ: (*Singing*) 'Join together, purge all guilt. Live life fully. To the hilt. Red-nosed Flotie in you we trust. Black Jack Scarron and the rest of us.'

SCARRON: (*Singing*) 'Join together. Go, go, go. Change conditions here below. Red-nosed Flotie in you we trust. Battered Grez and the rest of us.'

ALL: (*Singing*) 'Join together. Make it new. Who's invited? All of you! Grez and Flotie in you we trust. Black Jack Scarron and the rest of us.'

MARGUERITE: Bells!

(*All look at* SONNERIE *who has been dancing on the table. He is shivering violently. Trying to get down, he collapses and falls.* BRODIN *catches him and lowers him to the ground. They all gather round.*)

FLOTE: What is it, Master Bells?

TOULON: The plague cough and burn boils on his neck.

GREZ: He shivers in pain.

FRAPPER: And spits black bug's blood.

FLOTE: Is it the pestilence, Master Bells?

MARGUERITE: It can't be. Didn't you hear, sweet Bells? It's over.

ROCHFORT: The war's over but there's always one last arrow fired, one last gallant to fall though he shouldn't.

DRUCE: They go like this on the instant; cough, shiver, bleed, die.

SCARRON: Even the best.

BRODIN: Never cry quarter, Bells – fight!

(SONNERIE *shakes his right arm.*)

TOULON: Rest, Master Bells, save your strength.

FRAPPER: And you surely shall see the sun shine soon.

(*But* SONNERIE *continues to shake his arm.*)

FLOTE: I can't hear you, Bells . . . Quiet please, let Brother

Bells speak . . . Yes . . . you have a vision . . . you hear
the music of the spheres . . . see lakes and towers and
bells . . . their fragrance . . . one hundred thousand
bells . . . and beyond them a hundred thousand times a
hundred thousand ringing in the blue . . . Oh Bells . . . I
can't hear you, Bells . . .

(SONNERIE'*s arm drops. He dies.* MARGUERITE *sobs.*)

BRODIN: Ashes to ashes, dust to dust is a beggar poor bargain
but it's the only one we're given.

TOULON: His foot was as light as a four-year-old's. All those
who saw his holy dancing were changed, for in their hearts
he worked both weeping and rapture in one.

(TOULON *and* FLOTE *make the sign of the cross over*
SONNERIE. BRODIN *and* ROCHFORT *pick up the dead man
and hoist him on to their shoulders. Heads bowed, the other men
line up behind them with small handbells with their clappers
muffled, which they ring softly on each step they take. The light
begins to fade as the funeral cortège slowly crosses the stage to
exit Upstage Left.*)

MARGUERITE: When a good man dies, letters still come for
him. I want to pray but can only pray to my light, my dove,
my dear, dead Bells. It was over so quick, he was dead
before God got the news. Now you're gone what's Hell to
me? I'm punished sure. If there is life after death, why do
we have to die? My thoughts race round and round, going
somewhere to come back from nowhere. Bells, you've left
me a poor dizzard. Why didn't you spit in Death's face and
tell heaven to wait? I needed you more, you gap-toothed
gloak. Oh but stars, suns, moons, flowers, honeys could not
express my Bells. He was so sweet, so fair. A sad wind
blows. Black flags fly over Auxerre, Graverie and beyond. I
am already heart-sore for thee my heavenly Bells.

(ROCHFORT *enters Downstage Right.*)

ROCHFORT: Save me, Marguerite.

MARGUERITE: Save you?

ROCHFORT: I'm no longer amused.

MARGUERITE: Be serious.

ROCHFORT: I am. When amusement ends, my only defence

against boredom is hatred. The world's turning back again; perfectly organized and perfectly dead like poor dead Bells. And like Flote and the rest will be if they don't submit. The holiday is over.

MARGUERITE: Was that what it was, Brother, days of sun, days of freedom?

ROCHFORT: Summer warmth for plants and trees. Wind and rain for fish and dragons. Just another dream. It's time to unsheath my sword and flash it. I've told Brodin, I'm booting it free again. Leave with me, Marguerite. I'm a wrong-side nobleman but handsome – lofty brow, legs majestic. I know I'm conceited but what's my opinion against the mirror's?

MARGUERITE: You've a pretty wit and I've always preferred fake politeness to sincere boorishness.

ROCHFORT: Come close and save me, Marguerite, be my spur and purpose. I'll reinvent war, carve out an empire, tilt the world for you. Only come closer.

MARGUERITE: If I come any closer, I'll be behind you. I'm a woman who always lets her body go to her head. Oh, but your body's velvet soft. I feel the movement of your loins – my chuck, my chuck.

ROCHFORT: Save me and I'll pull down the pillars of the earth, eat your tongue, leave my teethmarks black upon your lips.

MARGUERITE: You'll be my Altar, my Vespers, my Mass!

ROCHFORT: Come with me! Live happy ever dafter!

MARGUERITE: Oh my mallard, I'll live dafter! . . . No, it wouldn't be right to come now. We owe Father Flote that loyalty.

ROCHFORT: 'Loyalty' – there's a fine word.

MARGUERITE: For loving friendship's sake we must stay for the Nativity he's set his heart on. When it's over we'll eat the world together. Just wait a little and I'll come.
(*She exits smiling Stage Right.*)

ROCHFORT: When you wish to see your enemy's face, look into a mirror. I wanted to reach the shore of the sea that has no shore and she talks of loyalty and friendship. Fine words, fine words. I never heard them in my father's house. (*He gets up and takes off his monk's habit to show he is wearing his armour and sword underneath.*) Marguerite, none but the brave desert the fair. I can't wait for any woman to come. (BRODIN *enters Upstage Centre putting the finishing touches to a banner, which he shows to* ROCHFORT.)

BRODIN: Do you like it?

ROCHFORT: I like it but I begin to smell the Crécy stink of defeat. We've swords to sell again, Brodin.

(BRODIN *lays out the banner on the ground to dry.*)

BRODIN: I've lost the taste for blood. Laughter's turned me soft. I've no more pride in the manly arts of war, sword thrust, axe blow. Like Antony, my god's abandoned me.

ROCHFORT: Never. You're Brodin. Whose name made whole populations flee? – Brodin. Whose voice was thunder? – Brodin. Remember how we fought south of the walls, died north of the ramparts and the morning light shining on bright armour? Man, man, there's work for us. It takes force to re-enforce order. Archbishop Monselet and the Civil Authorities will pay good money for our swords.

BRODIN: I'm corrupted. Before I could hire out to whatever side paid most – English, French, Swiss, no matter, I fought loyally for 'em all, sometimes in the same battle. Now I can only fight for right. (*There is the faint sound of a trumpet and a horse galloping away into the distance.*) There, hear it! I told you, it's the god Mars fartsing off, leaving me . . . He hasn't left you yet, Rochfort. You're still in his service. But you won't find it easy changing sides. Monselet and the rest won't just take an honest soldier's word he's turned turncoat.

ROCHFORT: No, they'll want proof. (*He takes out his red nose.*) Give it back to Father Flote. Tell him I'm taking up my old trade again. I have to be true to myself.

(*As* BRODIN *takes the red nose,* ROCHFORT *grasps his wrist and pulls him violently forward.* BRODIN *grunts with pain, a dagger in his stomach;* ROCHFORT *has stabbed him.*)

BRODIN: Rochfort?

ROCHFORT: A dagger in the gut-sack, Brodin? Tut, you'd never have fallen for that old trick in the old days. Your death is all the proof they'll need I've truly turned turncoat. At least I've spared you dying in bed, white hair, wet legs, beating toothless gums. Go die like a soldier, Brodin, whilst I live like a lord.

(*He exits Stage Left, playing his flute, as others are heard approaching Stage Right.* BRODIN *drapes the banner around him to hide the dagger.* FLOTE, TOULON, MARGUERITE, LE GRUE, BEMBO, FRAPPER *and the* BOUTROS BROTHERS *enter Stage Right.*)

TOULON: Father Flote, for those of us gazing up from the lower slopes there's a simple choice of tactics – submission or defiance. There's a pike under the reeds and its name is Monselet. Do nothing to disturb the water.

(BRODIN *tosses Rochfort's red nose to* FLOTE.)

BRODIN: Brother Rochfort's farewell. He's signed off, gone back to killing.

MARGUERITE: So, so, he couldn't wait for me to come. I thought he deserved me, but what man deserves any woman?

FRAPPER: He wasn't a pleasant peasant but he had a presence.

LE GRUE: Some people I can't see 'cause they're never there. But that velvet-hosened gent I could always see.

FLOTE: He had a wit and a way. We'll miss him. But he'll return. Meanwhile, we must practise our Nativity play: *The Birth of the Son of Light*. Brother Brodin, let's hear your piece.

(BRODIN *puts on the crown and his red nose.*)

BRODIN: In this Nativity I play Herod.

OTHERS: (*Singing*) 'Herod! He's Herod. The very devil of a Herod! Some think him God. Others just a sod. He's Herod! He's Herod!'

(*As they sing,* BRODIN *thumps up and down in a furious dance.*)

BRODIN: The Romans made me King of Galilee. What makes me a born leader is my desire to organize other people's lives and make them worse. My father was Herod . . .

OTHERS: (*Singing*) 'Herod! He's Herod. The very devil of a Herod! Some call him God. Others just a sod. He's Herod!

He's Herod!'
(BRODIN *finds himself dancing madly again.*)

BRODIN: . . . the Great. I've trodden in the footsteps of the
master. (*He smells his foot.*) Well, I've trodden in
something. The family motto was 'Do unto others – then
run'. I'm a man of peace. A piece of this and a piece of that.
But my father, Herod . . .

OTHERS: (*Singing*) 'Herod! He's Herod, the very devil of a
Herod! Some call him God. Others just a sod. He's Herod!
He's Herod!'
(BRODIN, *looking furiously at them, dances, but less
energetically now.*)

BRODIN: He once led Judah into war. We fought for gold! Gold!
Gold! Well, you think we should've fought for zinc?
Though I'm the son of Herod . . .
(BRODIN *dances even before they start singing.*)

OTHERS: (*Singing*) 'Herod! He's Herod! . . . Etc., etc., etc.'

BRODIN: (*Sinking exhausted*) I believe in free speech. When I
make a speech I never charge admission. We Herods . . .
(*He twitches his legs in the air in a token dance. The* OTHERS
laugh.)

FLOTE: I like it, Brother B., but the final collapse should be
more final. Comedy is funniest when it's most true. (*He
mimes* BRODIN's *dance.*) Make it more real, realler than real.
Otherwise you'll die the death.

BRODIN: (*Laughing*) But I am, Brother, I am.
(*As he attempts to get up, the banner draped around him falls
open to show the dagger and the wound. The* OTHERS *gasp.*)

TOULON: What is it, Brother Brodin?

BRODIN: A parting gift from my friend, Rochfort. Sent with
love.

MARGUERITE: I had his love too, it kills.

BRODIN: No reproaches, Sister Marguerite, for our murdering
friend. He's turned slaughterer again, so he slaughters. And
no tears for me, I've slaughtered too, in my time.
Cuirassiers at the ready!

FLOTE: Forgive me, Brother, I didn't know.

BRODIN: But I go out in joy, friend. I expected to die alone

85

screaming on some forgotten battlefield. Instead I'm dying amongst friends, in the midst of life. There's no loneliness or death in this dying. Only you'll have to play Herod, Father Flote, the very devil of a Herod.

BOUTROS ONE: What's happening?

BOUTROS TWO: I don't understand.

LE GRUE: Don't be blind. Death hangs in the air.

BEMBO: We lose another friend.

FRAPPER: Amid mist and coldest frost, Brother Brodin is singing his last sad song.

TOULON: No one will be as good as you, Brother. You were touched with such grace.

BRODIN: I had class. Lookee who's here. Death's come. Not enough time left to confess me, Fathers. I've lived like a man, that says it all. Lift me up, I want to face him. (TOULON *and* FLOTE *lift him to his feet.*) My regrets, Sister Marguerite, I never did rape you.

MARGUERITE: Another time perhaps. Would you like your sword in your hand?

BRODIN: No, a jest would be more fitting. This is a good one. Once when I was captured, the enemy commander asked, 'How many men in your army?' 'I'll never tell,' I said. 'Prepare the boiling oil,' he roared. 'Do your worst, sirrah,' I yelled back, 'I'd rather be boiled in oil than betray 34,635 men!' (*The* OTHERS *laugh.*) Oh it's good to take smiles with us into that last darkness; they light the way. (*The lights go down.*) Halbardiers advance! The show, the show! I can see it. The bright lights and the bright banners. Then the trumpet toot-toot-toot and drums up, up, up my heart and we're on . . . What's that you say? Crécy? We *did* lose at Crécy. Ah, now I know.

(*He falls dead in the darkness.*)

THREE

*There is a tremendous crash and shattering of glass in the darkness.
Lights up on the antechamber of Clement VI. The magnifying mirror
set at an angle Upstage Centre is smashed.* CLEMENT VI *steps out of
the adjoining room into the antechamber.*

CLEMENT VI: Behold I come forth in iniquity, back into the
world of dust, dirt, dung, carrion and fools. Who keeps
holy day for Judas? Cold days, sharp days, long nights
come apace. Save me, Lord. No, I'll not appeal to the
Lord. It's madness to put on gloves when one is stark
naked. If there's butcher-work to do let's not be coy
about it. Bring on the wolves, *arrrwaaaa.* (*He howls
like a wolf.* ARCHBISHOP MONSELET *enters, Stage Left, with
documents, and* ATTENDANTS, *who strip* CLEMENT.)
Now the plague has passed, we must immediately limit,
tame, subordinate, rule. Submission and belief, the twin
poles of the world must be restored. And quick, else they
acquire a taste for the other way. (*The* ATTENDANTS
massage his hands and feet.) When I heard you'd crept back,
my dear Monselet, I knew the danger was over. The last
time I saw you, your knees were beating each other to
death.

MONSELET: Holy Father, only he who survives is right.

CLEMENT VI: Don't just stand there, be of use. (MONSELET
helps with the massaging.) We've work to do. Christ's work.
First, increase the taxes on the clergy and loan Philip fifty
thousand gold florins for his war against the English. We'll
support his coming campaign to crush the Black Ravens by
proclaiming them anathema. In return, Philip will support
us against the Flagellants.

MONSELET: Many of your Cardinals are disposed to think well
of them as a new penitential discipline.

CLEMENT VI: Don't they see the danger to the Church of
allowing independent manifestation of zeal? More

important, what's to become of the most profitable function of the Holy Office – selling salvation – if men can cleanse themselves? If they're getting it free from the Flagellants we'll be forced out of the salvation business. Issue a Papal Bull condemning all Flagellants. You look graveyard grave, Monselet. Is there a thought growing in the brain that must lie behind that face?

MONSELET: Noses! Noses, Noses everywhere. Streets, squares, barns and halls filled with crazed Noses, thundering herds of Red Noses roaming the land like bison. Flote's Noses, Your Holiness.

CLEMENT VI: I appointed you Archbishop because you're free of the slavery of talent. Christianity is a system designed by geniuses for execution by idiots. Its continued existence proves almost anything can be made to work. Don't you remember, you sanctioned Father Flote's Red-Nosed Fools and I ratified the decision. A good decision. He's helped keep unrest down to a minimum; made men more readily accept their miserable lot. Flote's proved useful. A revolution never returns.

MONSELET: It's certain we gave him his chance. But you've often said, 'Give a man enough rope and he'll hang you.' Flote's joining with the Flagellants and Black Ravens.
(*The* ATTENDANTS *dress* CLEMENT VI.)

CLEMENT VI: I smell the sour smell of sour grapes. Whilst you sat on some fat mountain, Flote and his Red Ones stayed below fighting death to a decision.

MONSELET: Holy Father, you taught me only the weak are unselfish. As Archbishop I couldn't afford to be seen dead. I'm glad Flote stayed on my orders. It was proof I had not deserted my flock. But consider the man's power. I set Father Toulon as a Red Nose to spy for me and I've had nothing from him but insults. Father Toulon was a zealot's zealot on obedience, yet he's been turned in his turn.

CLEMENT VI: Because Flote loves with a full heart. He has all the makings of a saint. In other words – trouble. I take note of your warning note. Eye to keyhole, Archbishop. Report to me of Flote's activities. (*He puts on jewels.*) The centre

must glitter once more. We mark plague's end with
displays, tourneys, masquerades to celebrate the defeat of
chaos and a return to normality, order and symmetry.
The plague left them trembling but free
But man is too wicked to be free.
It is the nature of the viper to crawl and spit venom
And the nature of man to obey.
Submission and belief are the twin levers which raise me
    high.
Now I summon back the great engines of authority,
Rack, stake and gallows; palaces, courts and counting
    houses.
You strong leaders must leave your bed of worms,
You kings, high dukes, lords, judges and the rest
Adjust your gowns and crowns, sharpen your swords.
Charles of Bohemia, Casimer the Great, John of France
Amadeus, Green Count of Savoy, Dandolo, Doge of
    Venice,
Cantcuzene the Ottoman, Yussef of Granada, Pedro the
    Cruel and Charles the Bad,
Rulers of earth and sky, dissent is a sin.
Crush it and reimpose the three-fold chains of State,
    Church and Marriage
And quick, else they learn to like another way.
The remedy of disorder is terror;
Go break the spine of the world.
The plague was a time of tearful innocence,
Now a greater darkness falls
For we return to normal.
(*They exit Stage Right to wolflike howling.*)

FOUR

The howling changes to wedding bells ringing joyfully in the main square of Auxerre, whilst gallows are pushed in Upstage Left and three wooden stakes Upstage Right by GUARDS *in black armour. They exit Upstage Left and Right as* PELLICO *and* LEFRANC *enter Downstage Right.*

PELLICO: Marriage is a desperate thing, Lefranc. My bride-to-be can't even cook. I'll let a woman ruin my life but not my stomach.

LEFRANC: Thousands of men are married and even happy. The plague's gone. Our duty's plain. The Church insists we set an example. We remarry for money and heirs. Our new wives are rich – and breathing. We can't ask for more. As newly appointed Magistrates of Auxerre, we must restore our morality and fortunes.

PELLICO: But you have to like women inordinately to actually live in the same house with them. There're other things to life besides money. But then you need money to enjoy 'em. 'Gold, gold, gold . . .'

LEFRANC and PELLICO: (*Chanting*) 'Molten, graven, hammered, rolled. Chains of gold are chains that hold.' (*Solemnly chanting, they cross Downstage Centre to meet* CAMILLE *and* MARIE, *entering Downstage Left as brides with veils and small bouquets and* MONSELET, *in surplice and white stole. The couples kneel in front of* MONSELET *as the bells ring out again and he conducts a wedding service, though the words cannot be heard.* PELLICO *and* LEFRANC *put rings on their brides' fingers and* MONSELET *makes the sign of the cross over them.* PELLICO, LEFRANC, CAMILLE *and* MARIE *rise and the bells stop ringing.*)

PELLICO: It's tradition for bride and groom to smack a big wet one, kiss-kiss.

MARIE: Kisses cost money.

CAMILLE: No. Now all lip work comes free.

MARIE: Free?!

CAMILLE: We've lost our professional status, Marie, no longer honest whores, we've shrivelled to wives. Careers blasted on a 'love, honour and obey . . .' I could've been the greatest whore-mistress in Avignon, if I'd kept my mind on my body and my body under a man. Fame and fortune thrown away and for what?

LEFRANC: Respectability. They'll never look down on you again from a hole in the ceiling. They'll look up, Madam.

MARIE: And for respectability's sake we lose our self-respect. Men like you've always preyed on women like us. Before I had a business.

LEFRANC: Calm yourself, Madam. You've entered marriage, that's a business too. We're only interested in using your money, not your private parts. As husbands, we prefer the simulated enthusiasm of a whore to the dignified acquiescence of a wife.

PELLICO: Speak for yourself, Lefranc. I'll copulate till dry. I plan to spend the equivalent of two hundred florins a night on forbidden dainties.

MONSELET: Leave the higher-tariff items till later, Master Pellico. Content yourself with a quick kiss on the lips as is the custom . . . (*Drumbeats as* SCARRON *and* DRUCE *with two* GUARDS *enter Upstage Left and are escorted on to the gallows in chains.*) My Right Worshipful Magistrates, it's time to do your duty.

PELLICO: Duty? Since the plague left us, all that's left us is duty.

(*Nooses are placed round* DRUCE's *and* SCARRON's *necks.* LEFRANC *and* PELLICO *put on black hats. The drumming ends.*)

LEFRANC: The accused, known as the Black Ravens, come before this seat of Justice for greasing. That is, spreading plague pus to stimulate the pestilence which was a time of luxury for them. They did also cut the throats of the rich and entered their houses to rob them. We, the Magistrates of the High Council of Auxerre, do hereby solemnly pass sentence.

(PELLICO, LEFRANC *and their* WIVES *fall under a fusillade of old shoes, thrown by* FLOTE, MARGUERITE *and* FRAPPER, *as they enter Downstage Right.*)

FLOTE: Are we late for the ceremony? We mean to drink the happiness of the brides and grooms and sing naughty songs outside the bedroom windows.

MONSELET: You missed the wedding but you're in time for the funeral.

MARGUERITE: Archbishop Monselet, you're back, the danger must be over.

FRAPPER: You're lucky, Sister Marguerite, he'd never accept that from a smaller woman.

LEFRANC: We're hanging these men. They've confessed to being greasers.

(FLOTE *and the others turn and see* DRUCE *and* SCARRON *on the gallows.*)

DRUCE: Ladies, I've serviced you, do me a service now. Don't let 'em shovel cold dirt into my mouth. I've claimed so many with my sugar-scented breath. Oh, my fancy never died. I've been a rampant face-maker, fathered more into this world than I've ever taken out. Weighed in the balance, I come down on the side of life.

MARGUERITE: Ladies, he blows great horns of joy, the love-look is on him. Show him mercy.

CAMILLE: What's mercy's colour, size, shape, weight? What price mercy? We can't afford it. Respectability's cleaned us out. Hang him. Let him dangle.

DRUCE: I've never let it dangle, not ever, ladies.

MARIE: Take heart, hanged men have the mightiest erections. When you go limp, you go hard. Hang 'em.

FLOTE: Before you can hang 'em there must be a trial, lawyers, Inns-of-Court-men, arguing pro and contra. (*He puts on a lawyer's gown.*) No case too small, no fee too large. You prisoners are the victims of the grossest injustice and judicial corruption. Have no fear, your case is irrefutable. Just one question – what are you accused of?

MARGUERITE: (*Putting on a lawyer's gown*) Your Worships, *de minimus no curat lex* – the law does not concern itself

92

with trifles.

FRAPPER: (*Producing his dummy in a little lawyer's gown*) *De similibus idem est judicium* – in similar cases the verdict is the selfsame.

MARGUERITE: It's hard being a lawyer, lying awake nights worrying about your clients, imagining what they'll do to you if they ever get out of prison.

FLOTE: Your Worships, must we wheel out the bloody engines of Justice again, stocks for vagrants, whips for harlots, ropes, weights and brands for felons, knife and gibbet for murderers? God's put away His weeding knife and scythe, so should we. The power of forgiveness spreads like a garden; unused it recedes from us. Sun and sky plead for these men. The West Wind too. But speech is blasphemous, silence a lie; beyond the speech and silence, blasphemy and lie is another way. (*He calls softly:*) *Chick-chick-chick*, *sweer-sweer*, *toe-toe*, *cee-tu*, *cee-tu*, *tirruffi*, *tirruffi*.

MONSELET: *C–c–c–r–r–r–k–k*. The God of Mercy said, 'Thine eye shall not spare the murderer.' Hang 'em.

FRAPPER: Before your Worships do, I wish to bring vital new evidence to your attention. Your Worships, the accused have money.

PELLICO: Money? You show great skill, Brother Frapper. A Paris Inns-of-Court lawyer couldn't've put it better.

LEFRANC: Some lawyers know law, others know judges. There are few legal problems money can't solve. Father Flote, you should've mentioned this vital new evidence. We impose a harsher sentence now. A fine of five hundred gold florins will bite deeper than hemp rope. No protests, Archbishop, this is Juro Civil no Canno Juro.

MONSELET: Five hundred gold ones can purge rape and murder in a civil court but not vile sedition. These men preached equality!

FLOTE: No, they merely advocated forming a moderate Party of Slow, Lawful, Orthodox Progress – S.L.O.P., SLOP.

PELLICO: On the rumoured charge of preaching equality, we shall give you a suspended sentence – a week hanging by your thumbs.

(ALL *offer congratulations to* DRUCE *and* SCARRON.)

SCARRON: Rabbit-suckers, rather the Milky Way round my
throat, eternity in my ears, than SLOP. I killed the Fats
with the ferocity of an avenging angel.

DRUCE: Not me, not me, I was always a loving flounder, quick
to love, slow to die.

SCARRON: I loved too when I was greasing 'em dead. The poor
are like trees in winter, nothing green about 'em. To make
that part of mankind happy, I'd happily slaughter the rest.

FLOTE: Your Worships, torture's loosened his wits. Gentles,
never confess anything till you feel rigor mortis setting in.

SCARRON: No, it's time to hang me out. I'm one who missed his
chance. I failed. I broke the eggs but I didn't know how to
make the omelette . . . I dreamed, dream-wide of a
different ordered world, no will yielding to a superior will,
no blocks, knives, axes, swords. But I've seen the rich fall,
the priests run, the mighty tremble and that's something
better than Christ's palmy triumph on an ass entering
Jerusalem!

(*A* GUARD *pulls the lever at a signal from* LEFRANC, *and*
DRUCE *and* SCARRON *fall through a trapdoor, then are jerked
up high. As* FLOTE *and the* FLOTIES *bow their heads,*
PELLICO, LEFRANC, CAMILLE *and* MARIE *look up intently
at* DRUCE.)

LEFRANC: You're right, hanged men do have mighty erections.
See Master Druce's is hard and huge.

PELLICO: In truth, it reminds me of mine.

MARIE: That long?

PELLICO: No, that dead.

MONSELET: *Caw-caw.*

FLOTE: Sky dark as mud, God no longer tickles me *ooh-aah-ooh.*
The warm milk turns to vinegar in my mouth. The plague's
past but there's no light only a dark that sucks out the light
and my voice is a shout in a dream. Lord save me from the
hooded angel, the four-breasted bird, the shrieking flower.
Lord save me from the heaviness which is the end to mirth.

(*Drumbeats.* GREZ *and two* FLAGELLANTS *enter Upstage*

Right, chained and gagged and escorted by two GUARDS *in black armour.* TOULON *walks with them. The* FLAGELLANTS *are tied to the stakes Upstage Right by the* GUARDS. *The drumming stops.*)

MONSELET: Pertinacious heretics, you continue to disobey the Holy Father's edict. The stake is the only remedy for such disobedience.

LEFRANC: But it comes expensive when the authorities have to bear the whole cost of wood, rope and straw.

PELLICO: There's a good secondhand gallows going to waste.

CAMILLE: Every dutiful wife knows money saved is money earned.

(FLOTE *crosses and removes* GREZ's *gag.*)

MONSELET: Now they'll talk so much, their tonsils'll get frostbite. Where's your obedience, Father Flote? I speak for the Universal Church. Father Toulon knows.

TOULON: I know the sooner I never see you again the better it'll be for both of us when we meet, Archbishop.

(*He removes the* FIRST FLAGELLANT's, *and* FRAPPER, *the* SECOND FLAGELLANT's *gags.*)

FLOTE: Master Grez, I fear our friend Master Scarron has fallen through a trapdoor. He'd've hurt himself if he hadn't had a rope round his neck at the time.

GREZ: And we'll fry; fricassee'ed Flagellants. Father Flote, put away your Noses. There's nothing for laughter here. The divine evaporates. The brutal alone remains.

FLOTE: Never, we'll fight it down. Come, let's give 'em the play and save them – and the darkening world. Bembo! Le Grue! The play, the play!

MONSELET: First the Flagellants.

PELLICO: First the play. The frying can come later.

(*Beating his drum loudly,* BEMBO *enters Stage Right with* LE GRUE *pulling the small portable stage Stage Left.* FLOTE, FRAPPER, MARGUERITE *and* TOULON *hurriedly exit Downstage Left.*)

BEMBO: Oyez! Oyez! Christ's Clowns present a brand new activity. It is our version of the Nativity. The Christ child is born into a world much like this one. Will you laugh or weep when you see what's said and done? . . . (*The* AUDIENCE, *including* PATRIS, SABINE, ARTISANS *and* PEASANTS *enter shivering upstage centre between the gallows and stakes and join* PELLICO, LEFRANC, CAMILLE, MARIE *and* MONSELET.) Oyez! Oyez! Our new play is called *Christ and Kings*. And shows Herod, Balthazar and the rest. Who were there at the birth of sweet Jesus. Our first scene is at Herod's Court. He is a king, he seems to loom. But he couldn't find his way out of an empty room.

(*There is a fanfare as* TOULON, *in robes and a red nose, enters Downstage Left as the High Priest Noncios and places a throne opposite the portable stage whilst* BEMBO *exits behind it, Stage Left.*)

TOULON: I am the High Priest Noncios and I command you all keep silence for one of the rulers of the earth – Jude et Rex Israel – King Herod!

(*Another fanfare. There is a scuffling behind the portable stage curtain, muffled curses and finally* FLOTE, *as Herod, crawls from under it, crown and robes askew and red nose gleaming. As the* AUDIENCE *laughs,* FLOTE *comes down off the stage and crosses to the throne.*)

FLOTE: I'm a king, so why can't I make a good entrance, Noncios? Kill whoever's responsible. Why do people take an instant dislike to me, Noncios?

TOULON: It saves time, Sire.

FLOTE: Now hear, all you serfs, vassals and slaves, I, King Herod, decree the word 'wicked' shall be replaced by the word 'noble'.

TOULON: A far-sighted decision, noble Herod.

FLOTE: Kill him!

(LE GRUE *stumbles in Stage Left.*)

LE GRUE: I want to make my home in your kingdom of Judah.

FLOTE: This man is an idiot!

LE GRUE: I'm also blind.

FLOTE: A blind idiot – that's different. What do you do?

LE GRUE: Nothing. I'm a nobleman.

FLOTE: Noncios, make him a government minister with the rest of the nobility. (*His crown falls over his head.*) Plagues of

96

Egypt, I'm blind!

LE GRUE: You're blind? I'm the one who's blind. You wouldn't last a day blind. It takes character!

(*He exits Stage Right.* FLOTE *recovers.* TOULON *gives him a sceptre.*)

FLOTE: Who else comes to my door this morning, Noncios?

TOULON: Well, Sire, there's a Tinman, a Strawman and a Lion outside looking for a little girl with ruby-coloured slippers.

FLOTE: Who isn't, Noncios, who isn't?

TOULON: Yes indeed, Sire. There are also three Kings from the East.

FLOTE: Kings are my sort of people. Open the gates and let 'em in.

(TOULON *claps his hands and the richly gowned figures of* BEMBO *and the* BOUTROS BROTHERS, *complete with golden crutches, enter, bowing, Stage Left.*)

BEMBO: Most noble Herod. (FLOTE *hits* TOULON *with his sceptre.*) I'm Balthazar, this is King Jasper of Taurus and this Melchior, King of Aginar. Twelve days ago a bright star appeared in our heavens. We followed it here to Jerusalem, for our prophets foretold it would lead us to a newborn babe who will be the Saviour of Mankind, a King of Kings.

FLOTE: Why wasn't I informed, Noncios? I spend a fortune on informers and all I get is information. A King of Kings you say?

BOUTROS ONE: It's why we came bearing gifts in hope he'll remember us in his coming days of power.

BOUTROS TWO: It never hurts to be on the winning side. And all the signs confirm this babe's a winner.

FLOTE: On your way back, tell us who the lucky little bas– fellow is. So I can pay him homage.

BEMBO: A noble thought, noble Herod.

(FLOTE *hits* TOULON *again as* BEMBO *and the* BOUTROS BROTHERS *exit Stage Right, bowing.* FLOTE *chuckles.*)

FLOTE: Idiots. They're all idiots. When they return, kill them. But only after they've told us where this kingly babe is hiding. I promise you his reign's going to be very short.

One king in Judah's more than enough. Why is it me who always has this trouble? Messiahs, Saviours, one-legged kings. Did you see, Noncios, those two only had one leg apiece? Odd. First thing I noticed.

(*As* FLOTE *and* TOULON *exit Stage Left behind the portable stage, its curtains open to show a traditional nativity scene in the Bethlehem stable with* FRAPPER *as Joseph,* MARGUERITE *as Mary and a doll as the infant Jesus in the manger.*)

MONSELET: Anathema! You mock God. For the authority of kings, yea even Herod's, comes from God, and in mocking them you mock Him.

PELLICO: Mirth and jollity's not good enough for them now. They want to make us think.

CAMILLE: That's not fair.

MARIE: We didn't come here to think.

LEFRANC: See, they pour their black pitch on the Holy Family. That stuttering simikin's not Joseph and that licentious nun's never been a mother or a virgin.

SABINE: My mother was a saint in her own lifetime.

PATRIS: We worship the ground she's buried under.

(FRAPPER *and* MARGUERITE *continue the Nativity.*)

FRAPPER: I–I–I'm J–J–Joseph. (*He picks up the Jesus doll and loses his stammer.*) I shiver. Is it dread of Herod or the cold?

MARGUERITE: I'm Mary – yes, I *have* been a virgin and a mother. Not both at once, of course. That only happened to the Virgin Mary – that's me . . . Stop complaining, Joseph. It's all your fault. I leave you to make the travel arrangements and look where we spend the night. And stop shivering. Our blessed laughing babe will soon warm us. He brings us light and love and hope. He's a token of God's tender care for mankind, coochie-coochie.

MONSELET: I've heard enough! This is a nest of pertinacious heretics all. In defiance of the Papal Bull October 20th, 1349, the cursed Brethren of the Cross, the Flagellants, remain unrelaxed heretics, and are hereby handed over to the secular arm for punishment. Burn 'em.

LEFRANC: Burn 'em.

(*As* FLOTE *and the other* CLOWNS *rush in Downstage Left and*

Right, still in their Nativity costumes, light plays over the FLAGELLANTS.)

FLOTE: I'm bent double.

MARGUERITE: It's only clowns like us that speak of love, laughter and the life everlasting.

TOULON: God is strictly neutral.

GREZ: Stand easy, friends, it's much easier to die well than to live well. Fiercer fires than these scald my soul. We've been tricked, sold dogmeat for mutton. We embraced pain when we should've tried to eliminate it. You were right, friend Flote. God's a joker gleeful at the sight of men staggering under the axe blows of life. He doesn't want our suffering.

FIRST FLAGELLANT: Now he tells us!

SECOND FLAGELLANT: What's it matter? This is my last chance. No more cries, *ahhh-ahhh*. I've got a thousand last words I've never used. 'Miasma'. That's one and 'harmony' and 'sunset'. Last words are important. Makes a man's name remembered after. 'Sunrise' – there's another . . . 'star-stretched' . . . 'pear-shaped' . . . 'Zion' . . . *ahhh-ahh.*

(*The light flickers fiercely over them as they burn, writhe and die to loud drumming as* CLEMENT VI *enters in dazzling white, Upstage Centre between the burning* FLAGELLANTS *and hanged* BLACK RAVENS. *He is accompanied by four* GUARDS, *the* HERALD *and a bejewelled* ROCHFORT. *The* AUDIENCE *and* FLOTIES *kneel. The flickering lights on the* FLAGELLANTS *die down as* MONSELET *quickly crosses and kisses the ring on* CLEMENT VI's *finger*.)

MONSELET: Now spoil, rack, pierce these Noses with your cold iron, Holy Father.

CLEMENT VI: Archbishop, your power yields to one greater. Dwindle to your normal size. My new secretary, Count de Rochfort, has told me all I need to know about the Floties.

MONSELET: Your Holiness, why do you have a cynic like this Rochfort as your secretary?

CLEMENT VI: Because all my secretaries become cynics in the end. I thought this time, why wait? Fathers Flote, Toulon, Sister Marguerite, come.

(MARGUERITE, FLOTE *and* TOULON *stand before*
CLEMENT VI.)

MONSELET: But Your Holiness, 'Count' Rochfort used to be of
their company, a Red-Nosed Flotie.

MARGUERITE: Now he's joined the new generation of Judas
that walk the earth. You had the chance to transcend
yourself and be my very perfect knight. And you gave it
up – for what?

ROCHFORT: Everything. I entered my father's house another
Joseph and it was all mine. How my family embraced me
when I returned and how they wept when I kicked them
out. No man forgets where he buried the hatchet. Thanks
to His Holiness, I've estates, position, power. And I gave
up nothing except a little love. No, I still love.

FLOTE: Talking of love isn't love; it's the acting of love that's
love.

MARGUERITE: Go spill your guts out in a field for not waiting
for love.

ROCHFORT: Love I can buy on any corner, market-day.

CLEMENT VI: I've found me a fine ravaging wolf, eh? I feel safe
with his treachery and greed. It's honest, God-driven men
like you, Father Flote, I can't trust. You live by no rules
except what's in your heart. Without rules and laws, every
man becomes a law unto himself. So I must give your
company strict rules and orders.

TOULON: What need we of rules and orders? There's no buying
or selling here as at Avignon, saw-teeth and hook-claws. We
hold all things in common. No man is wronged where no
man is a possessor.

CLEMENT VI: So, Father Toulon, you've changed horses in
midstream?

TOULON: Yes, the old one drowned, Holy Father.

CLEMENT VI: Unless you submit, Father Flote, I'll grind your
Noses into dust along with the Flagellants and Ravens.

FLOTE: What must I do, Your Holiness?

CLEMENT VI: Please the populace with passing shows; relax
them with culinary delights – meringues, jellies and
whipped cream. But give them no meat to chew on.

FLOTE: But the Lord is my consuming fire. He lights my soul; eyes and tongue aflame. I'm still combustible.

(CLEMENT VI *takes a water bottle from* ROCHFORT *and pours the contents over* FLOTE.)

CLEMENT VI: Obey or die.

FLOTE: I'll not hang or burn up my friends, Holy Father. The dream fades, the rain's colder, the stone's in my throat. The Floties will submit.

CLEMENT VI: Then continue with your show. Make us smile and forget it. (*He crosses himself.*) Pray for me.

TOULON: Why do you cross yourself, Holy Father?

CLEMENT VI: I've crossed everyone else. Rise, my children, and see the birth of the Christ child.

(*The kneeling* AUDIENCE *rises.* MARGUERITE *rejoins* FRAPPER *on the portable stage and* FLOTE *and* TOULON *disappear behind it as* BEMBO *enters Upstage Right, banging his drum.*)

BEMBO: Oyez, oyez. In a stable the infant Jesus chose to lie. Amongst the poor who never die. They've never lived so how can they die? But now, Joseph and Mary once more take their bow.

(*He exits Upstage Left whilst* MARGUERITE *takes the baby from the crib.*)

MARGUERITE: Lookee, look how my sweeting laughs. Oh he's a prince divine.

FRAPPER: (*Taking the baby*) All mothers say that about their sons. He's comely, full of Godhead. But why call him Jesus? It should've been Ezekiel. That's an easy name to forget. (*A star is dropped from the Flies and hangs in front of the small stage.*) Strange. I've just seen a bright star and it's still morning.

MARGUERITE: You've been drinking again.

(BEMBO *and the* BOUTROS BROTHERS, *as the three Kings, enter Upstage Right bearing gifts. They kneel in front of the portable stage.*)

BOUTROS ONE: Hail Lord, I bring this cup of gold in token you are without equal.

BOUTROS TWO: Hail Lord, I bring this cup of incense in token we bow down and worship thee.

BEMBO: Hail Lord, I bring this cup of myrrh in token you'll restore mankind to life. (*They put the three cups on the small stage.*) Only remember in Thy coming years of triumph, kings paid you tribute. We bend knee to you so your followers will bend knee to us after. (*The baby gurgles agreement; they rise.*) We promised to see Herod again. If that royal clodpoll had more sense, he'd be a halfwit. When he's said 'hello', he's told you all he knows. Just take up your child and flee to Egypt and you'll be safe.

(*The* THREE KINGS *exit laughing, Upstage Right, whilst* FRAPPER *and* MARGUERITE *frantically scoop up the gifts, baby, crib and straw and follow them. The small stage curtain falls as* FLOTE, *as Herod, rushes on from behind the portable stage with* TOULON *as Noncios.*)

FLOTE: Out, out, out! Bring me my cleavers, chisels, meat hooks. Not one king returned as promised – there's friendship, there's gratitude. Where do I find this miraculous babe, this future king of Judah? Where? Everywhere! Ah, you have to get up pretty early in the morning to catch Herod.

TOULON: About twelve noon. You must be careful, Sire. Even the shepherds are beginning to talk.

FLOTE: Influential shepherds?

TOULON: Jewish shepherds.

FLOTE: Intellectuals! Let 'em talk. Wheel in my knights! (LE GRUE *and* BEMBO *enter Upstage Right dressed like the Guards, only their 'armour' is made of paper.*) Sir Knights, there's a traitor risen in Judah who usurps my authority. Go seek out and kill all the newborn males in Zion. (MARGUERITE *enters from behind the portable stage as a poor woman in a tattered shawl, cradling two dolls in swaddling clothes.*)

BEMBO: We're men of noble blood, Herod, not butchers.

TOULON: 'Happy shall he be that taketh and dasheth thy little ones against the stones.' Psalm 137.

FLOTE: 'The little ones die or you die.' Herod 138, 139, 140.

LE GRUE: If it's a choice between them and us, it quickly

dwindles down to us. I see the necessity of it.

BEMBO: Another plague has entered the world. It's wrong but we are under orders.

(*The* BOUTROS BROTHERS *enter Upstage Right as Guards in paper armour, carrying a large wicker basket filled with dolls in swaddling clothes which they tip on to the floor.*)

MARGUERITE: Don't take them from me! They are my babes, my joys, my lovely days.

(*But* BEMBO *and* LE GRUE *take her dolls and throw them with the others. As the parody Guards move towards them, they make the sounds of babies crying and screaming.* MARGUERITE *joins in the babies' terrified howls whilst the* AUDIENCE *shouts.*)

SABINE: Stop! Are you men?

PATRIS: Spit on your orders!

MONSELET: We were promised soothing syrup.

LEFRANC: But see what they give us.

PELLICO: Where are the jollies?

MARGUERITE: Don't cry, my little lambs, my lambkins. If you had lived you would have learned to love your rulers for the way their softest whisper is obeyed like a shouted command. But you only lived long enough to feel their sharp swords. (*She slowly kneels.*) Lamikins, lamikins, go down, go down. All go down. Babylon go down, Ninevah go down, go down with me.

(*The cries of the 'babies' finally stop.*)

CLEMENT VI: It isn't funny!

FLOTE: No, it isn't funny. In the days of pestilence we could be funny but now we're back to normal, life is too serious to be funny. God's a joker but His jests fall flat. (*He takes off his red nose.*) It isn't funny when they feed us lies, crush the light, sweep the stars from the heavens. Isn't funny now inequality's in, naming rich and poor, mine and thine. Isn't funny when power rules and men manifest all their deeds in oppression. Isn't funny till we throw out the old rubbish and gold and silver rust. Then it'll be funny. (*He tosses the red nose on to the ground.*) Holy Father, I can't submit. I tried to lift Creation from bondage with mirth. Wrong. Our humour was a way of evading truth, avoiding responsibility.

Our mirth was used to divert attention whilst the strong ones slunk back to their thrones and palaces where they stand now in their saggy breeches and paper crowns, absurd like me.

CLEMENT VI: Stand aside from that man. He is anathema!

(ALL *shrink back instinctively from* FLOTE *who takes off his paper crown and throws it to* ROCHFORT.)

FLOTE: It's hard to die. Only the young talk of that easy leap into death. I tell you, when Death comes a-knock-knock-knocking the best course is to run. But just sometimes you have to stand your ground and dance!

(FLOTE *slowly moves forward, arms stretched wide, feet rhythmically stamping as he begins dancing the Greek Kolo.*)

CLEMENT VI: Stand aside from that man. He is marked for death.

TOULON: Flote, you're a great fool. But now's the time for final choosing. On the one side, the Holy Fathers, Archbishops, Goldmerchants, Herods and Kings. On the other, the Fools, male and female, Father F., Sister M., Bembo, Le Grue and the rest. Reason can't help me choose. So I choose without any reason other than my taste for good company and my aversion to bad. (*He takes off his red nose and throws it on the ground beside Flote's.*) Once I was hot for obedience and scorched the earth with fire. Father Flote showed me how to illuminate it with kindness and mirth. You're a mad zad, Father Flote, and I never learnt to play a tune on my head or rub my knees together, like the 'Human Grasshopper', but I'd rather rot, lose my life than your friendship. Though I'm no dancer, I'm dancing with you.

(*Stamping his feet rhythmically, he takes his place on the right of* FLOTE. *Arms on each others' shoulders they dance as* MARGUERITE *takes off her red nose and puts it with the others.*)

MARGUERITE: Pig-gelders, you'll never be the men your mothers were. I could've built cities, pleasured a thousand strong men. And shall I die with this undone? But you can't saw sawdust. It's over. We lived the vision, rolled back the stony heart a little and the glory is measureless. Nothing to lament, let's pierce the circumference of Hell and dance! (*She takes her place on the left of* FLOTE. *They put their arms on each other's shoulders and, with* TOULON *on the other side, dance, as* LE GRUE *comes forward and throws his false nose with the others.*)

LE GRUE: I'd like to stay with you but I'm blind. I'm a blind coward, you see. Lived in this darkness, frightened to face that darkness. You understand. Must love you and leave you. Feet, do your stuff. Run. Feet! Feet! (*He starts to dance.*) No, run feet, run. Feet?! Feet?! Look, Ma, I'm dancing!

(*Despite himself he links up with the line of dancers as* FRAPPER *puts his false nose with the others.*)

FRAPPER: I just thought a thought but the thought I thought wasn't the thought I thought I thought. Thanks to Father Flote I'm no longer a shy fly in a flue. I can say 'boo' to all of you.

(*He links up with the dancers as* BEMBO *throws his nose on the pile.*)

BEMBO: Why wait till my hair turns white? I choose my death. Three days in a hot oven and perhaps I'll rise again.

(*He links arms with the line of dancers whilst the* BOUTROS BROTHERS *throw their noses on the pile.*)

BOUTROS ONE: Don't leave us out.

BOUTROS TWO: We're the professional dancers.

(*They throw away their crutches and join up on either end of the line of dancers. Arms linked, they circle the stage, stamping rhythmically, whilst the* AUDIENCE *clap their hands in time to the dance. At the climax the* FLOTIES *come Downstage, shouting and laughing.* CLEMENT VI *raises his hand.*)

CLEMENT VI: Let them taste it!

(*The* GUARDS *raise their crossbows and fire. There is the magnified sound of dozens of arrows in flight. The* DANCERS *are hit. Some cry out, others gasp as they spin, stagger, fall and finally lie still. Only* FLOTE *remains miraculously unharmed. He looks down at the bodies all around, then steps forward smiling.*)

FLOTE: This reminds of the condemned man who was being taken up the steps of the gallows and suddenly burst out laughing. 'You mustn't do that,' said the executioner, shocked. 'This is a solemn occasion.' 'Sorry,' said the prisoner. 'But I just can't help it. You see you're hanging the wrong man . . .' How long is it good for a man to live? Only as long as he does not prefer death to life. I've seen men die sitting, lying, dropping on their knees like bulls, but never upside down, standing on their heads. One must have sport even with death.

(*He kneels and slowly levers himself up till he is standing on his head.* CLEMENT VI *raises his hand again.*)

FIRST GUARD: Your Holiness, we can shoot a man in the back, but not standing on his head. It isn't natural.

(ROCHFORT *takes the crossbow from the* FIRST GUARD, *aims it at* FLOTE *and fires. There is the magnified sound of a single arrow in flight, followed by a thud as it hits its mark.* FLOTE *topples over, dead.* ROCHFORT *plays a funeral air on his flute and the* AUDIENCE *silently disperses Upstage Centre.*)

CLEMENT VI: Build them no monuments; no funeral urns, no civil rites must mark their termination. We have no further use for them. Let the Floties sleep forgotten, their light, ashes. They have never been. Sand out their names. Yet to be nameless and have lived, showing how men should live, is a true remembrance. The Canaanite woman helping Jesus lives more happily without a name than Salome with one. Better the nameless good Samaritan than Herod, these poor clowns than Pope Clement VI. Father Flote thought he'd failed. No man fails completely who shows us glory. I live, rule, drink blood. Say a good word for me, Father to Father. Wind blow the poppy seeds over them and us, *aaaaawwh.*

(*He howls softly as the lights fade down to a spot on the pile of noses.*)

Heaven is dark and the earth a secret
The cold snaps our bones, we shiver
And dogs sniff round us, licking their paws
Monsters eat our soul

There is no way back
Until God calls us to shadow
So we rage at the wall and howl.
Go down, she said, go down with me.
World go down, dark go down,
Universe and infinity go down,
Go down with me, *aaaaaaawwh*.

White mist and a single spot on the pile of false red noses Downstage Left. The ghostly voices of FLOTE *and the others are heard in snatches of conversation and sounds from the past.*

FLOTE'S VOICE: Lord, as this bread upon the table was in separate grains and being gathered together became one good thing, so let all men and women be gathered together into one family . . .
(*Sounds of eating.*)

BRODIN'S VOICE: I'm for deep pots, wide pans . . .

TOULON'S VOICE: Ah, what food these morsels be . . .

MARGUERITE'S VOICE: Don't eat so fast, Le Grue. It's the first time I've seen anyone get sparks from a spoon . . .

LE GRUE'S VOICE: Neat's tongue! Why aren't there neat's tongues. . . ?

FRAPPER'S VOICE: The seething sea ceaseth seething . . .

BEMBO'S VOICE: Passable . . .
(*There is the sound of* SONNERIE'*s bells.*)

BRODIN'S VOICE: Marvellously well told, Master Bells . . .

SCARRON'S VOICE: There's no Heaven or Hell but if a man has good fortune and lives well that's Heaven, *caw-caw* . . .

GREZ'S VOICE: By suffering, men find their true strength *ahhhh* . . .

FLOTE'S VOICE: Every jest should be a small revolution . . .

BOUTROS ONE: Don't leave us out . . .

BOUTROS TWO: We're professional dancers . . .

ALL: (*Singing*) 'Join together that's the plan. It's the secret. Man helps man . . .'

FLOTE'S VOICE: It isn't funny. God's a joker but his jests fall flat . . . (*The magnified sounds of arrows being fired.*) No, it isn't funny. It's serious . . . Oh, but, oh, a world ruled by seriousness alone is an old world, a grave, graveyard world. Mirth makes the green sap rise and the wildebeest run mad. Not the mirth born of anxiety and fear but the mirth of ·

children and sages, the laughter of compassion and joy.

TOULON'S VOICE: Father Flote, this was to be a résumé of what we said when we were alive. You never said that.

FLOTE'S VOICE: I should have done.

TOULON'S VOICE: Father, we're about to be ushered into the Creator's presence. No old jests. If He asks how we got up here, please don't sneeze and say, 'Flu.' We've other matters to discuss.

MARGUERITE'S VOICE: I want to find out how He came to make such a botch job of everything.

FRAPPER'S VOICE: I'm going to ask him if he meant giraffes and camels to look like that or was it an accident?

BEMBO'S VOICE: God's up for judgement.

(*A single clear trumpet note in the distance and tinkling bells.*)

TOULON'S VOICE: That's us, Brothers.

LE GRUE'S VOICE: I can see a light.

BRODIN'S VOICE: Father, we were famous but do you think we'll live?

(*Ghostly laughter.*)

ALL: (*Singing*) 'Join together. No weak link. Must keep trying. Else we sink. Join together all of you. Pierre Frapper and blind Le Grue. Charlie Bembo and the other two . . .'

FLOTE'S VOICE: God, count us in.

(*The sound of their voices grows faint as the spot on the pile of noses fades out.*)